Poems by Harold
A Life Lived

by

Harold Ebright

Compiled by Sandra E. Weiss

Version 1.1. Updated 17 June 2021.

Version 1.0 originally published 13 May 2021.

4sweiss@gmail.com

Produced by D.X. Ferris @ 6623 Press Invitational.

Proofreading by Brendan Halpin.

Cover design by Christy Carmody.

ISBN 978-0-578-89723-3

Table of Contents

Notes on Style and Content

This book collects poems by Harold Ebright.

The poems appear as Harold wrote them, with his references, neologisms, salutations, formatting, usage, and punctuation intact. He labored to make these poems look the way they do.

Harold used language eccentrically. He used some words of his own creation. That is the way he wrote. This is his work, as he created it.

Harold Ebright signed almost every poem. He seldom used the same *nom de plume* three times — or two — in a row. Sometimes he signed off as "H.E.Bright," sometimes "H E BRIGHT," sometimes "h e bright." (period), sometimes "h e bright," and sometimes as "H. Ebright." Sometimes he signed off with a short message or directive — depending how he felt that day. Those variations in his pen name represent part of the narrative he left behind. So each closing has been preserved, as a record of his process, and as a possible clue to what he thought and how he felt in the moment.

The following images may reflect limitations and feature imperfections from the source files.

I hope you enjoy this record of Harold's life's work.

Photograph Captions

Page 6
The family, long before us. Harold's father and mother, Sam and Ruth, on the bottom. His sister Pearl on the left, brother Herbert in the middle, Harold/Dad on the right, before joining the Navy. He followed his brother into the military when he was 18, so we believe this was before then.

Page 7
Harold on a submarine. He spent 11 years in the Navy. Several poems refer to his time on a sub.

Page 8
Harold and Miriam's wedding, October 1948, with their parents, Ruth and Sam and Anne and John. Dad's first wife, my Mom.

Page 14
Harold, early days, I believe just after left the Navy. With his Mom (our Grandma Ruth), his sons Bob and Steven, before I arrived.

Page 15
Harold with Denise, his second wife and love of his life, and Kim's Mom, early 1970's. Bob was in the Army, Steven in the Navy. I was in my teens, and Kim was a toddler. He was the happiest during this time, which may be why few poems were written (the ones I did know about but did not find). He was busy living, boating, weeding, trips to Hawaii and cruises, buying/selling houses to move the growing family.

Page 24
Harold in a suit, 1983, going somewhere special.

Page 46
Farmer Harold in Swiftwater/Cresco, PA. This was his yard to mow, grow the garden, and watch deer and other animals. This was his Paradise.

Page 126
Harold and Mary, Dad's 3rd wife, around 2008. As the poems reflect, Happy Times in Paradise.

Page 182
Their land in Paradise, what he left behind when he got sick but fought us all to go back to. He did sell the property when he moved to an independent apartment nearby.

Page 234
Harold the farmer, in his element, in Paradise, but by himself. Lonely times.

Page 300
The end, with girlfriend Jean, taken about a month before he passed over. Jean was with him the morning he was taken by ambulance to the hospital. He arrived DOA, dead on arrival, at 84 years of age. He always said, "Kid, you don't get out of here alive." But no matter how much he prepared us, it was still such a shock – we somehow expected him to outlive us all.

Acknowledgements

How does one say thank you for making something impossible possible?

So many people came together to make this book happen.

First there is the person who said, "Just do it," an author, writer, business owner, stock aficionado, and friend, Donna.

Donna facilitated the process by passing me to Darren Paltrowitz, another amazing writer/author and blogger.

Darren connected the dots by referring me to the best hand-holding, patient, and knowledgeable publisher, D.X. Ferris.

Ferris introduced me to Christy Carmody, who created a great cover.

Thanks to my dear friend Janet, who listened for hours on end as Dad modified, amended, and revised the poems that were so important to him.

Enormous thanks to my brother and sister, Bob (Wendy) and Kim (Dennis) for believing, listening and encouraging me along the way.

And to my husband Joe, who listened endlessly to the minutiae of drafting and redrafting.

Also kudos to all the Train buds, Banking pals, and Hood gals for your continued support.

And last, to the writer of these poems: Harold, Dad, who I promised long ago that his work can and will be available to readers.

To all who made this happen, thank you thank you thank you. Your encouragement has been so, so appreciated. You enabled this book to be completed.

It is real.

— **Sandra Weiss, May 2021**

The Promise

by Sandra Weiss

This is a preface and not a forward. Or something like that.

My father wrote poems. This book collects most of them. It represents one of his major goals. He wanted to be published. The volume in your hands fulfills a promise from me to him.

Never, never promise to do something and then throw away what you need to do that something. Dying is not easy – especially for the living. When our parents pass, we are left with the years and years of their and our lives to save, or dispose of. It becomes our choice, or our responsibility. My father wrote poetry for many years. Most of them (all?) were not very good, by my review, but I am not a poetry aficionado, so they might be very good. I will let you, the reader, decide.

When it came time to go through his personal belongings, I found many of his poems. But they were the recent ones. I knew there were more. How would I know he would file them (the first of how many years of his poems) between his years and years of tax returns? Why would anyone leave pages of personal poetry there? Perhaps he thought whoever (me) was going through his personal items would be interested (nosey) to look at his reported income and find the older poems. Or maybe he thought they weren't good and didn't really want them saved…. We will never know.

So it's not really my fault that, after hours and hours of throwing things away, I would even think to look through tax returns. If this had been the first or second box we went through, then maybe I might have looked a bit. But when it was the third day of box after box of papers and "stuff" (my favorite word), what was left was mostly garbage-bound – even if it shouldn't have been.

Did I consciously reason that what I was seeing was the poems I had promised to safeguard? Looking back, had I realized they were the poems, I would have saved them all. But I didn't. I had found many in his office, archived on numerous thumb drives.

So what we have are the poems, most of them written after 2008, which I believe represent about half, or more, of his poetry. As his children, we were born long after his childhood. We have no knowledge of his earlier poems and life. But we were there for his late 60s and 70s, until his death at 85. Those years remain in our hearts, and in the poetry, as a tribute to him and his life.

As you read, you should understand some things about my father. First about the poems, then about him, as we knew him. The poems all seem to have two or three undercurrents of meaning; one being very sexual, adult stuff about love and yearning. Sometimes it was difficult to listen to him read thoughts that had no interest to me, and as his daughter, I really did not want to go there with my father, my Dad. I don't think he realized they were personal like that. He just wanted anyone listening to understand his thoughts... I think!

He would spend hours, days, weeks on one poem. So that when he announced it was finished, it was nothing like the first draft. While reading them, he would lose me; their meaning was not clear, but convoluted, or complicated. But he was my Dad, so I listened.

The second theme was always time. And as he aged, I could see it was about his diminishing amount of time. Now as I read them, and as I advance in age, I see how one could fixate on that aspect. Unfortunately, we all age out, and we die, but each person manages that in their own way. His was to write about it.

The third theme, the undercurrent, was his love of the earth. He was also ALWAYS connected to the ground, to the dirt, by gardening, farming, fishing, boating, and weeding (one of his favorite hobbies). If he wasn't working, he was outside. In retirement, he had a little side business fixing lawn mowers, which he always did in the garage, outside.

All of these are reflected in his writings. Combine them with his humor about life, and what you get are the poems. Finally, since he was married three times, one can see how his relationships influenced his life and the writings.

In May 2015, Harold passed to the other side. His third wife, Mary, had passed in March of 2012, and he was never the same. Soon after he caught a very bad cold, it turned into pneumonia. And only because of Kim, his youngest daughter, did he recover.

He lived over 100 miles from any family and did not want to move. (He wanted us to come live with him – part of this appears in the poetry.) We, of course, tried very hard to get him to be closer, and extended several different choices. When he was sick, not long after Mary passed, he was in the hospital for over a month. Then, because we believed he was best somewhat near us, he was moved into a quasi-assisted, almost-independent-living facility in Westchester, New York.

Within months, he grew restless and staged a "coo," as he called it, to escape back to his home in Pennsylvania. The poems in 2013 reflect this restlessness. Luckily, he was able to locate an independent facility and live near his large home, which was not near to us. The poems in 2014 seem to show how his independence made him happy.

In less than two years, he would pass away, frustrated by getting older and not having a wife or anyone to care for him the way he required. In my and brother and sister's defense, we tried very hard to find a compromise, but he was a stubborn Libra. He wanted what he wanted. And he never considered any of the ideas we had after his stay in Westchester — except to be near what he called his Paradise. One wonders, without Mary, whether it was truly the heaven he remembered — or had hoped for.

I will end the book with the poem he was working on when he passed, which was read at his funeral.

See, Dad: I am keeping my word. Here is your book of poems.

ONCE IN A LIFETIME

by Harold N. Ebright

I got patted on the head, by a teacher. And she said, "It is a nice poem you read," when for the class I recited. That was 75 years ago. and wouldn't you know that had started as a glow got poetry in me ignited.

I garner words in my mind, half asleep at night, as a poetic instinct instrument. But thoughts get lost and far out of sight, scrambling for a writing implement. By the time I put pencil to pad (Now this is sad) I'd forgotten what kept me there. With this spark lighted, and me excited, a blank mind now sits with a stare. Who said life is fair, and I'm mad.

Well anyway, I call myself a POET, So wouldn't you know it, Curses for verses can't find my pencil. It's unreal, how I feel could someone, from me steal, and ruin my prose? Perhaps a stencil would work, I suppose.

I began to think and tried using pen and ink, but when writing this way, I was faced, I must say, that everything written must be double-spaced. In ink nothing can be erased, so the pages fill too quickly. I am so resentful if someone took my pencil, as he who played this trick, must surely be a dick, and sickly.

In finding other implements to write with, and I've never been lazy, so I tried to paint my thoughts for fun. The words were smeared and as I feared the letters were hazy, and I didn't know where I'd begun. The drippings ran and my every plan only made me more crazy.

Then I tried charcoal from the hibachi (Rhymes with Carachi) But as a fool! It seems I'd forgotten the coals had to cool. Burnt all my fingers, and the heat and hurt still lingers, What a joke, and worst of all the pages all went up in smoke.

Don't laugh, if you can't feel the pain, sit back and hear the rest as I explain. Threw water on the fire as a necessary desire to save some burnt ashes that might remain. This might have been hot stuff that one might have called "Porn in the buff," but nothing now can ever be the same. What is truly insane Is how I have to explain, with nothing to gain.

Though my poetry is usually humble, this mess was quite a jumble, and as a prelude for my personnel ashes, (When I die) later will testify, that nothing lasts forever, Said someone, very clever, and perhaps writing memoirs, is more than an endeavor. — Whatever, whatever.

As my tale can sort of tell, why one should never dwell, or continue to write his epitaph.

In the time it takes to live, and enjoy the means that give, no matter what route you employ.

Take the time to weave your bower, for just so many minutes in an hour could take years to grow that special sweetest flower, and extend exert your special power.

Have a pursuit and find the route that takes you to the sweetest fruit. Stand aligned and you will find, being the first, to slake your thirst, and know their is peace in a quenching shower, hour by hour, never cower, and never sour.

Only then could you say, "Whose life was it, anyway?"

Harold Ebright
7/9/13

CHAPTER 1

A Story

and

The Early Poems: 1984 - 2004

Since Harold left behind so little documentation of his life, it was amazing to find a story about his childhood — although this is, as he was, a bit out of the ordinary. (Some would say peculiar; others say unique.) But in this there is humor, and that is what he and his life were about, finding humor in everyday things. Many of his poems display this quirky sense of humor.

A STORY

How could it be like yesterday, if yesterday was sixty-five years ago? Sure, it's amazing how the time disappears. But to be reasonable, so much time in a person's life indicates an awful lot of living. Month, year and day by day, a lot of existing in all those years. And it puts me now at least in the Old Man category. But I'm more!

And yet, it seems like only yesterday that an eleven-year-old, on his way home from some adventure, happened into a bewildering situation. And just facts, no fabrications. How easy it is to pump up an event, or embellish a situation. I must have told this story a thousand times though the ensuing years. Always the same, and always with the sense of awe that this memory brings, and the goose pimples.

It started out as a faint whirring, way off in the distance, and as it slowly got louder and louder, it got stranger and stranger. A sound coming from the west in front of me was like nothing I have ever heard. I couldn't see anything except a mile of tree leaves in a line, and dense green obscuring the horizon.

It was late August, and light was fading as the sun fell towards the West. Must have been around seven, seven thirty, and the coming dark wasn't going to help. The sound was getting louder, and this thing was somewhere over my head now. For an eleven-year-old, everything new was a learning experience.

How fantastic to be so formidable when only too soon, the summer's break would come to an end, and then back to school. As I remember, and there were not too many previous years to draw on, but I do remember that school was a pain in the butt. Had it not been for those tall windows and a seat close by, my opportunity for continuously dreaming might have been wasted on the whole boring repetition of learning.

To me, it was a complete turnoff, as most of the stuff sunk in the first time. Standing there under God only knows what is overhead, and from previous years' memory, I knew the teacher would ask, "What did you do on your summer vacation?"

Well, this thing up there, coming towards me must be a helicopter. Something we've only seen in the movies, and so low in the sky, that it should be here, but with the trees. I still can't see it. I will, I will. I'll be able to see the gondola, the propellers, maybe even someone waving to me from a helicopter window! Wow! it sounds low. It's right at the tree tops.

I have to remember everything, and this experience is sure to get me a lot of attention. To a grown person, it's called respect. If your parents weren't military, or your family wasn't able to contribute heavily to the school, then you were not considered much in the community, or the class.

Those were just before the war years when things in Europe were heating up. People were being persecuted without mercy, and a tyrant named Hitler was ravishing and dancing all over Paris. In those days it was good politics to keep your nose clean, especially if you were Jewish. The world needs a scapegoat, and things haven't changed for the last two thousand years. Is there anything new? The need for some notice, for an eleven-year-old would surely be feather in a needy cap. I grew up as a small child in a predominantly Italian neighborhood, and my religion was Jew Bastard.

Everyone in our neighborhood called us that. It was the times and the world was in dire straits. Respect was non-existing and the world was a follow-the-leader mentality, no matter how bad a situation presented itself.

It wasn't until I was a seven-year-old, the year 1936, that my religion "Jew Bastard" became a slap in the face. I suddenly realized that we were victimized, the poor white from a lesser part of society. You didn't have to be Jewish to know it was a sore token of ill respect from the so-called better classes. Just profanity, and fighting about it, getting into an argument was a waste of time. Kids learn from their parents before they learn it on the street. Either way, growing up is not easy, no matter what the situations are, at any age.

Well, here it comes, and I see it. A window under a lighted dome. In fact, the whole dome is lit, and it is a large circular object much smaller than a dirigible could be. And a person is leaning on the glass shading his eyes from the glare in the dome. It's moving slowly over my head, and he's looking right at me.

It is not quite darkness behind it and there are many mechanical objects underneath, but no balloon, propellers, no gondola, and strangest of all, no noise. What a total disappointment.

And how come, in just seconds of time, it got completely black? Darkness came in like two seconds, and the thing just completely disappeared. How could that be? I feel strange, like my head fits on backwards.

Oh well! Nobody is going to believe this one anyway. I wouldn't even bother trying to convince anyone that something flew over my head shinned a light on me. I did get scolded for coming home later than usual, and not having a legitimate excuse for missing supper.

The Early Poems:
1984 - 2004

As noted, his early poems were not retained. There are several from 1984 through 2004. This is prior to being with his third wife, Mary, when the majority of the poems were written. They retired together to the Pocono Mountains, to their Paradise. When they first moved, it was much more rural and he was in his element, farming, fixing lawnmowers and more importantly, having a wonderful woman to take care of him. She passed away in 2012. Then he became ill, and he was admitted to a hospital in Westchester, nearer to us. Although less than 100 miles away, it was a different planet to him.

In 2013, when he was in Westchester, bored and not able to take care of a garden or drive or do things independently, he had a lot more time, and the poems reflect a lot about those difficulties. Then he moved back to Pennsylvania, to the area he considered home. The remainder of poems were completed there.

I would like to say he was happy; however, when reading the poems, I always seem to come to the conclusion he had such a difficult time with the aging process. I would guess many have this dilemma, as we age, but it seems he needed to describe what he was feeling.

Perhaps the poems can assist in how we each come to grips with our own aging. And maybe that is why he made me promise to put these together, to be read by you.

Finally, a few definitions:

Moosh

A black cat that lived outside for a few years adopted Mary and Harold and lived the remainder of his older life in their home.

Applesauce

Outside the house was a very large apple tree. It was very large. In a storm its main trunk split in half and looked like it had died. Then, in the spring, the remaining small trunk grew, and within a year, it bore fruit, and then apples came for the next number of years, although fewer and fewer each year. He loved that tree, its sheer size, the shade it provided, its presence. Many of his poems reference trees and the applesauce he made.

Two Acts of Earth

She's a wounded hurting mother earth
    are we to let her die
Is carelessness and overbirth
    to sever every tie

Of life (so dear) it started here
    the line had no reversal
How bright the future and so clear
    "this is it" no dress rehearsal

To later the finger, facts are real
    it points so hard to bear
With just the chance she'll never heal
    where will we get our air?

And water is undrinkable
    will circumstances share
The burden is unthinkable
    an earth without a spare

Who to blame to bear the shame
    for the coming strife
Can we mother? Wear the name
    "responsible for life?"

A voyage world at home in space
    that twice can't occupy
It glides within the swirls to chase
    the diamonds in the sky.

Though exitless she still remains
    locked up in place and sore
A victim of so many pains
    are sins and strains of war

Is it mother you despair

    from all the hurt and pain

What warrants change and huge repair

    might help you yet retain

The earth (she shouts) the gift to man

    to propagate her race

Develop (she says) best you can

    your intellect and grace.

She echoed loud to no avail

    how can you so abide

All locked upon a serpent's tail

    that rattles when you ride

The first act is a hundred wind

    to set the man up straight

To blow upon some mortal sin

    is just and natural fate.

So normal acting earth rebounds
    in sending stormy strife
She will not separate the sounds
    of prayers and promise life

Is fire, smoke and all to choke, earth
    debt that comes to even
Remains on earth of little worth
    as blessed goes with heathen

It's hard to tell how could one dwell
    on a possible stormy purge
But hardened fearful man is well
    and in wisdom few did merge –

With clouds as placid waters rise
    and sunshine spreads new dreams
How godly is that man has eyes
    to vision all he deems.

Like shining stars of heaven's fate

    was sprayed upon the green

If man can learn to appreciate

    the earth he can redeem

Mother's wrath is in accord

    for nature to evolve

A thousand winds her next reward

    for problems we can't solve.

H E BRIGHT

11-86

HALSTUF

I'm restless in this rock hard chair,

in googled eyed, computed glare.

Amusing lights, blipping curses

groping for some missing verses.

From daughter Sam, these PC gifts

will open natural genial rifts.

Life was peaceful, calm, serene

but never more, says this machine.

Oh! kin of mine, the harm you've brought

Redundant is your simple thought.

How could you, lovely daughter Sandy

Clog my drain with a simple Tandy.

Plugging voids of life's demand

a leaf alone can never stand.

You save the tree for future seed.

This kind of love is all I need....

H.E.BRIGHT 3/19/94

A Sword or Cross

I have nightmares with repeating dreams
In a strong new royal existence
Where ghostly shadows control, what seems
Like a conscience without resistance

God must forgive my terrible need,
This commitment i have with gold.
To defend debauchery, lust and greed,
Is why this dream is told!

As i reign i sleep unresting
Under a weighted righteous crown
Of accusations i'm contesting,
As feeble charges found

I cannot sleep with horrible dreams
This regal splendor, is sorted scenes
Of wealth and power that time perversed,
With tainted blessings, royally cursed.

I'm in shining armor, i'm very officious
Dreaming, i lead this tirade.
Disgruntled followers, so suspicious
They form a vindictive parade,

Of creeping shadows with obvious ties
That have put my schemes on hold.
With blatant charges, envious eyes
Have tarnished all my gold.

Fools want to know, of my vision's glow
And greedy expectations.
Their nagging pressure, needs to show
Filching aspirations.

Where once there was eden, fenced
And a peaceful place to dwell,
Ungratefully righteous time commenced
With blessing come from hell.

With magic lantern in my grasp
I should have knelt and prayed.
As a wished -or genie in the flask
Has now turned, and decayed

This gnarly old tree, where evils grow
With flailing limbs, that fears
An emerging shadow's eerie glow,
As a sinner's vision rears.

With my eyes opened, retinas bulge
On a wretched scene, i must divulge,
How fragile threads of life, so dear
Are threatened now, in dread and fear

Squinting to see, though wrinkles dim

That shadowy figure, staunch and grim

Has arms upraised, posed and steady

Holding something, all too ready.

Tears blur my focal plane.

Can what he carries cause me pain?

Cursing my eyes, i have to know

"shadow, are you friend or foe?"

A distant threat is not a menace,

And a bible in his hand for my penance

Would be a blessing, and my reward.

But oh god! Dear god, not a sword.

I've never prayed or called your name

Is it too late now, and all in vain?

If on my knees you make me stumble,

A severed head will surely humble

Perhaps I'm safe, and the blade i fear
Is a book of prayers. My sins to hear
With royal logic, let this king decree
An atonement possibility

Lord holds this life endearingly,
If a vision's blade is nearing me
Without compassion, let it fall.
For all the blessings i seek after all.

Are nightmares and terrible strife
Here to alleviate troubles in life?
Are good intentions to make amends
Enough to change how a shadow sends,

Blessings from god, and blessed we are
In our being, perfection by far
Is only he, forgiving sinners who pass
There is not realm without amass

For royalty, must also humble.

When he shakes the world, we all stumble

Into his blessings, so that strife

Can give new meanings for life....

h e bright

4/97

Yolanda And Mary, Mary And Yolanda

They bought a little piece of land

with a tiny house to share

knowing that every grain of sand

is magically aware

that a precious fertile tract of earth

is waiting to be sewn

with all of their creative worth,

in sharing what they own.

With any being that contains

 respect for nature creeds

it simply shows why love retains

a passion for animals' needs.

From two special women, I'd better explain

how humble lifetimes led

from an unending pocket-book drain,

to Karma, beautifully spread.

From two strange souls, warmth reflects,

as blessings on many abodes.

Easing the burden of many rejects,

it strengthens troubled loads.

He the provider, and a simple shack

chose two special girls, I swear,

with ridged rules for giving back,

the laws of loving care.

Says "why isn't everyone sharing

their blessings in this my world."

They hear of warnings blaring,

feeling spears to the heart being hurled.

Oh! "These two women are crazy"

Says the neighborhood babbling teens.

Never having a chance to be lazy,

benefits the soul, not the jeans.

A creature asking "why are these things"

might chance to lose his claim

when nature favors all her beings,

in choosing a top for the chain.

Beings, able to share with creatures

on this planet, staying alive.

was the answer from four legged teachers,

when questioned on how to survive.

A life is generally wrought,

doing penance on earth

as a gift for the soul is being taught.

In essence, saving the worth—

Of an animal neglected

came here without hesitation.

Hospitable love is reflected

as beneficial inspiration.

For understanding how to trust

when instincts are to run,

is knowing when a share is just

and a meal away from none.

A gift of faith expands

in simply knowing the needs

of those who never demand,

or expect rewards from deeds.

And with appreciation they succumb

for handouts on display,

when birdseed, corn, or a single crumb

is considered as "grand buffet."

Though two simple sisters can't agree
that sorrows come from greed,
and helping someone tenderly
improves the human breed —

Through all of us, god's gifted creatures
flows a tincture of ancient albumen.
As limbs extend far, to the reaches
of why it is, we are human.

Surmounted preposterous crests
a simple reason they don't wear
a badge of courage over their breasts,
having to prove they care.

As an accomplishment that couldn't spoil
complacency for all the toil
is a share of love, all of it free,
returned as blessings, so willingly.

H. E. Bright
1/2003

Gene Root Stock

A walk on freedom's bridge to where

The tunnel ends in light.

And bless a life we live to share

The dawns from darkest night.

Exploited people's damned intellect

Subjected to genocide burns.

A forced migration, lives and respect,

With haunting nightmare returns.

Made paupers, the lot of Europe's lore

Condemned as just existing.

In a world removed, expelled to explore

New ventures, and to cease resisting.

Innocent prey severally indexed,

Assailed for wanting their own.

Forced into acceptance, utterly perplexed,

Being ethically, prejudiced prone.

Persecuted minorities, in stoic protest.

Say your prayers, flee or die.

To perilous ocean trips, they regressed

For preservation, do they lie.

Foreign cities welcomed a lucky few

And being poor and hungry, was healthy.

The greens they ate, as cheap easy stew

Made the haunting dreams to be wealthy —

The irritation that stoked internal fires,

And the need to exist, are their stories.

As anyone knows, strangled desires

Make certainies other than the glories-

Of a selected few, from whatever lands

Traditioned to succeed and thrive,

With compassion, is how one understands

That existence, means staying alive.

Good "gene root stock" and intellect,

Insures for future generations,

With past memories, cautious respect,

Are for avoiding supplications.
(begging)

Kindness has no gender

As the essence of love is learned

In a world filled with splendor.

Odds are lessoned, "for getting burned"!

h. E. Bright

2004

CHAPTER 2

Times are Good in Paradise:

2006 - 2010

When Harold retired (he never actually stopped working), he and Mary (and her sister Yolanda and her Mom) had some houses renovated in a small town in the Poconos, Pennsylvania. The Township was named Paradise. The houses were on 5 acres, and he found his heaven, his paradise. By 2006, they were part of the community, had many friends and his beloved tremendous garden and working garage to fix lawnmowers and repair anything for anyone. Many of the poems are whimsical, presumably because he was busy and content.

Many of his poems made reference to nature: his garden, trees and being outside. That is who he was.

Is There Time

1

An awakened morning, has one opened eye

    On a clock's hand dictating change.

The lapsing time, scurrying bye,

    Confuses a day we arrange

2

What matters, is clock time compression,

    Fast minutes have suddenly appeared

And accepting these hours expression,

    Could exasperate moments revered.

3

At a fantasized treasure time rendered pace

    Intrigued from what it seems,

As enjoyment, while the moments race,

    With visions and outrageous dreams.

4

Seems that lapsing times, the years that grew

    Contingent with everything,

Were wound one time, before anyone knew

    About tensions, in a tight clock spring.

5

Trying to lengthen an hour's mass,

    Stretching days on which to rely,

Readily hampers the minutes that pass,

    And stresses out times to comply.

6

Yesterday becomes tomorrow,

    As time speeds by in haste,

In today's flash of sorrow

    Are the joys squeezed out in haste.

7

Cut and pasted are the past years filed,

    As those special enjoyed times,

On whose years, time has smiled,

    For observing caution signs.

8

On a dime is the measure

    Of a hyper perplexing rage,

Where frequent stops for pleasure

    Are enjoyed at every stage.

9

However in rushing the passing years

    Timed by sequenced signs,

Were often filled with somber tears.

    For those who cross the lines.

10

Where themes like vice are often spun,

    Tried scenes ran clocks at slow,

Too often requesting a setting sun

    To stretch the afterglow,

11

When minutes can hang like angel hair

    As the jewels of hours past,

Are the gems of seconds to really ware

    And make memories made at last.

12

From a backward contemplated course

    To justify the pace,

Where it could have been, without remorse

    Had left unseen without a trace,

13

And were those years, a flash of youth

    Like steps in a marching parade,

 A progressive connection, defining truth.

    Life is a complex charade.

14

Of compressed segments, tried and tested,

    And having come this far,

With so much spark, so much time invested

    Now reviewing where we are.

15

Yesterday's tomorrow, that dawning line

    Where most is yet unseen,

Is a guide on a rarely glimpsed sign

    Of an afterlife in between,

16

An inevitable end, unarguably true,

    Known actions tied with remorse

With pre-asked questions, like "What is new"

    In preparing for a second course....

H E BRIGHT, 1-2006

A Matter of Fact

1

Awoke the morning, opened an eye

    As a clock hand pushes advance.

The lapsing time, scurrying bye

    Competes for my day of chance.

2

For odd intriguing moments to last

    In the thoughts I've yet to scheme

As confirmed unreasonably vast,

    These ones I dare to dream.

3

The continuous strange times elapsing,

    Squeezing moments compressed,

Converting the hours collapsing

    Guaranteeing my daze, distressed.

4

My ticking clock passage, now slowing

    Once wound long ago, oddly brings

On the times of cautiously flowing

    Tensions, as of tight clock springs

5

Grasping for hours not lasting,

    To add on times in splendor,

Pushes the days faster passing,

    And rushes those left to remember.

6

Yesterday effects tomorrow

    Days, if the times are not wasted

Squeezing the joys from sorrows,

    Leaves the sourness only tasted

    (not swallowed),

7

Invested in the years of lives

    As a blink is on passing times,

Relayed to above, when comfort thrives

    On confessions in spiritual rhymes

8

And visions, hanging like angel hair

    As jewels of moments past,

As gems to remember, so many can share

    In the memories made to last.

9

Even when moments with sadness spun,

    And the times run scenes too slow,

And requests get denied from the setting sun,

    Not to rush the afterglow.

10

On a dime are timed treasures

    Enjoyments in this modern age,

Too frequently these embarrassed pleasures,

    Get displayed from every stage.

11

To navigate a rugged course,

    Seen converging in many places,

Best, without the tense remorse

    That leaves ungrateful traces.

12

Lived about the strange and longing

    Convinced that my passing parade,

Tired of so many years, belonging

    To anything but a charade

13

Survived the hectic rushing years

    Of rules and somber signs

All filled with salty saddened tears

    And crisscrossed scarring lines

14

  Compressed in segments, lived so hasted

    For these times to have this far

With sparks and gusto, we cut and pasted.

    Proving by far, who we are!

15

Yesterday's tomorrow as a sign

    Of what does it all really mean,

For today, to remember, "toe the line"

    For an afterlife is perhaps unseen.

H E BRIGHT
2010
bet on it?

LIMERICKS

by H.E.Bright

Remember that man from Nantucket

   had a large member; No one could suck it

   So awfully racked with grief,

   did he stand on a cliff,

   with dismay for the Gay, did he chuck it.

My sister, by law is Yolanda,

   for whom I could never be fonda.

   With her sister in tow,

   to the stores do they flow,

   Saving money, they say, But I wonder!

For meat there in Laos they cry

       Expensive and rare do they buy

       for the shopping is found

       running loose on the ground

       Keep yur dog tied up, near a Thai.

     A girl named Jerry wanted a vegematic.

     to deal with some critters in the attic

     She thought, with one blow

     Scared as hell they would go!

     For the hole in the floor she got static.

There was Mary and her pussycat, moosh,

     She has animal characteristics, a hairy bush.

     Feeding creatures, every kind

     With these thoughts in her mind,

     That someday they'll all kiss her tush.

In writing these Limericks, my head hurts.

but my passion for poetry brakes,

all the rules of rhyme

considered tacky for the time

That are wasted vexsationists, flakes.

The Story of Jason....

There was once was a very damp fellow

Named Jason, who sweated a lot

and the reason he's wet,

Is, he runs like a jet,

as the story develops a plot.

A very young JASON, of old

unwillingly runs from the fold

turned his water to salt,

It wasn't his fault

    in this terrible flee from the scold.

Ran Jason who sped up his race

noisome sweat did rattle his pace

with these beads, and his cross

He is so far off course,

    from the droplets that run down his face

Jason isn't exactly a tree

felled partly as time was to flee,

no roots to affirm

had he branches, they'd burn,

full of ashes and brimstone debris..........

Seems the tale might suddenly clear

"A long time ago" says the year

a man ran abrupt

from the time is corrupt

alleging his life and his fears

Saline drops of sweat and tears

are arrears gathered in fault

"Sodoms" race of the few

participants who knew

about futures in pillars of salt

2006

An Angel's Dilemma

1

Old man winter, exceptionally bold,

    Ignored her suggestion "Time to fold"

Proceeds to season his icy cold,

    Impedes all reason to release his hold.

2

He cares not for my opinion,

    A stressed angel indicates.

And from his cold dominion

    Insists that spring hesitates

3

As flapping ruffled wing feathers tire

    Fanning icy winter nights,

She calls on Prometheus, God of fire,

    To warm cold frigid flights

4

Now heated hearths, cause eaves to drip,

> Hanging spears tipped with sunlit gold.

On gentle breezes, as the months slip

> New calendar pages unfold.

5

She instigates, and proudly protests

> The delay in brightening skies,

With strong anticipation suggests,

> An impatience for winters demise.

6

To skip this season's frozen blight,

> And pass February without delay,

She flaps her wings with all her might,

> And Marches right into the fray.

7

A generous sun now, melts dirty snow

    Calming exhausted rages,

Instilling in poets, a tender flow

    Of inspiration, to green all stages

8

Our angel does exceptional things

    For our lives are charmed and sunny,

Entirely precious as the green she brings

    Is other than for greed and money

9

In simple terms, an angel decides,

    Where nature's bounty is applied

And with resourcefulness provides.

    For nature's luxury was never denied.

10

With all of alteration

   In every changing season

A master planned creation,

   Giving humanity, reason.

H E BRIGHT

1/17/07

To All Men of Physics

Cause you see the blazing light
As all the cosmos placate light
When squeezed the atoms blink and die,
Resolve this theme but never lie.

Oh blastmis sends a nova's woe
Unchaste do all the senses flow,
Plasmas strewn, neutrino's bound,
Does penetrate our sacred ground.

So stretched defined as basic matter,
Specks so fine as Higgs, no fatter.
Pulled from blasting stretched beyond
Existence haunts the cranial bond.

A sight of abject knowledge gore

Unequaled vast majestic pure,

Beseech you thus of tended brain,

Leach your knowledge. Save our strain.

Dangers weigh as posed genera,

Pray the blight does get no nearer,

Of special daunt does harm impend,

Bolster man's impending fend.

Of those grants, as flowing rivers,

Purge the way a throne delivers.

Win a martyr's stance record

Float this ship and all aboard.

H.E.Bright,

2008

The Years

1

Live a January seasoned cross,

    Live valued love to cherish loss,

Live borne of every chased desire,

    Live on, hearing angel choir.

2

Life is winter shedding the tears,

    Life is, of dart pointed frozen spears,

Life is too warm a Valentines day,

    Life is seasoning, blown away.

3

A wakening purges an icy stream,

    A stressfully tolerant latent scheme,

A tenacious primal warming trend,

    A compelling, springing, greening blend,

4

That warmed March wind sings cool refrains

    That echo from blossoming daisy chains,

That sound of eager teen requests,

    That amplifies song in tender chests.

5

In living with many questions rise

    In life are realities, blind disguise,

In twisted truths, in knowing cares,

    In how and in our future shares.

6

As months, as years of many pasts,

    As destiny chooses, as timing lasts.

As an arbiter of superficial plans,

    As if committed, as measured spans.

7

To April, showered hearts are known

    To March on flowered paths, sown.

To know of karma, to love with tears,

    To answered prayers, too overcome fears.

8

On questioned once, on pretense here,

    On valued breaths, on year by year,

On vibrant pulsing, on hearts replete,

    On dowered answers, on sum complete.

9

May is enthralled, love grows,

    In June are passionate friction glows,

In July are times a vibrant blush,

    In Augured hearts royal flush.
    (priest-soothsayer)

10

To sinfully age in consummation,

    To tolerate, tease shared humiliation

To pass without a heartbeat's miss,

    To earn the comfort years of bliss.

11

August seals a time of expose

    September chose the parting rose

  For precious latent memories fold,

    Will pass to striplings turning bold.

12

October fests in sunset's truce,

    November dines of feasting goose,

December, marked by holy fears

    To mediate forgotten years.

13

Epics spun with silver threads,

    Epic memories most of all.

Epics gathered on timeless beds,

    Epoch, plants the fall.

14

Once, two by two were spaces found,

    Once came full circle headlong bound,

Ones spade to breaking crusted ground.

    Ones hearing sacred angel sound.

15

These precious genes of gilded tastes,

    These seeds of life worth growing.

These fertilized with golden wastes,

    These, of his all knowing.

H E BRIGHT,
1/08

A Trail Tale

1

An odd tale, from a wooded trail,

    An encounter with fate will unfold

From a forest lane came sounds of pain,

    Made a true story here, being told.

2

A Mary did strive, running, keeping alive

    Doing that nature suggests.

Forsaking a calm, was a sounded alarm,

    Of surprisingly strange requests.

3

It had begun, on an exercise run,

    Hearing strange noises very queer.

Shortening her pace, for here in this place

    Were sounds, something crying, oh! dear.

4

In wood timbers tall, seasoning fall,

    Came a terrified baby's wail.

A heart wrenching cry would not deny,

    Problems, on trotter's trail.

5

Paused in her track, Mary looked back,

    Her ears turned like radar honing.

The crying so badly, has now, turned sadly,

    To sobs of pathetic moaning.

6

In heavy brush, greenery lush

    Was a shadow of something quite small

She pinpointed sound, and seemed to have found

    Two eyes on a tiny gray ball.

7

Preciously slow, out from branches low

    Came a pathetic injured rat

Then with a sigh, realized rodents don't cry,

    The rat was a small kitty cat.

8

Wish for the best, you probably guessed

    It almost ran out all nine.

Picked up so tender, knew God was the sender

    Says, "perhaps I can make her all mine."

9

With fate as a blessing, only guessing

    Lost and completely displaced

To have everything desired, as guidance required

    A trotter with lovely embrace.

10

In soft fluffy fur, fears turned to purr,

    Nestled now close and secure.

As a saver found, now homeward bound,

    With blessings and everything more.

11

This tale is written, of a strange kitten,

    Though his cries were a serious wail,

For a young cat, a difference is that,

    A stub is there instead of a tail.

12

A disturbing shakeup, was part of his makeup,

   When a no tail pussy was born,

So hard being tame, for the pranks and shame,

   And getting lost made more forlorn.

13

She ran with a quest, nestled close to her chest,

   Was a furball of pussy cat lost.

When looking for mother, his one love, no other

   She decided, he wasn't just tossed.

14

A shame for little no name, no one came,

   She looked, no one even phoned.

He became sad, which made him mad,

   Knowing, he's not even owned.

15

With animal handouts, this Mary stands out

    Enjoys feeding animal needs

Any four leggers, on two legs for beggars

    With corn bread, corn whiskey and seeds

16

So he gets weary, knows only Mary,

    With no tail and no covered tooch.

An owner not found, no claim'er around,

    Says "I'll keep him, and I'll call him Moosh."

17

Have given up knitten, She says for this kitten,

    And it is best for our liking.

We two agree, a home is the key,

    He can stay if he gives up hiking

18

At home now, this house, is free of the mouse,

    I'm an owner no longer in charge.

He struts around proud, every rodent in shroud,

    And his pride has expanded to large.

19

For a splendid male comes the end of this tale

    And fifteen years, from the heart.

Though minus of tail it has never meant fail,

    It was never an integral part.

20

Mary matched complete, as is heaven replete

    For some charming words of a song

A love resounding, voiced astounding,

    And Moosh can do no wrong.

h e bright.
2/2008

Why Do Poems Rhyme

From fakir pates, come aura's glow,

    In imaged mental mime,

    As supple vision's thought bestow,

    In gracious words of rhyme.

As onions ring a central core,

    In symmetrical satisfaction,

Scenes in poem's tiers explore,

    Justifiable abstraction.

The chosen word so needs a choice

    To blend as precious thought.

A sculpture seeds the chiseled voice

    For options dulcet sought. (pleasing-nice)

Harshly spoken whines distort,

    In words of contradiction,

Smoothing lips sway firmly wrought

    Sweet rhyme in a sought rendition.

The bleeding heart has a rhythmic goal

    To soothe a bodies drama

Beating in synch with mind and soul

    Can smooth ill rhyming trauma.

To read a poem of question marks,

    Thoughts leading a mind astray,

Exist unseen as natures quarks.

    Exasperate the lay. (poem)

Who sees contextual playtime

    as soft spoken verse

Consensual as May rhyme.

    With no need to rehearse.

Exceptionally dear are works ending near,

One enjoying words by a poet.

Here, with the sheer fear of thoughts unclear,

Often end too confused to know it.

H E BRIGHT 4/2008

Our Mother – 1

1

A single mother, planet earth
    Cares for all decedents,
Gave more than love and birth,
    A taste for independence.

2

Gives this single troubled mother
    Cause for a covenant decree.
For our conspiring with one another,
    Has fears to let us be.

3

In suffering, has this metaphor
    Staid underfoot for millions and more
Dedicated, devoted, she sacrificed for,
And taken for granted.
    This theme will explore!

4

For protection mother's maternal desires
 Shinning from a stars durability,
 Tempering burning greedy fires
 Of human insensitivity.

5

On an elliptical voyage of mystical thread
 Warmed in her golden breast
 Spinning reddened, vowing to shed,
 Portions of our blatant unrest.

6

 Embarrass meant as ringlets glow
 Suggesting reckless sin,
 As sympathetic tensions show,
 A race that cannot win.

7

Nurture began on mother's earth

    In bountiful dedication,

She never considered that strains of birth

    Could cause eradication.

8

Because humanity spawned bogus plans,

    As predatory assaults,

Our greedily contrived survival scams

    Exemplified our faults.

9

Considerations sparsely planted,

    Sewn of mockery's recourse,

With blessings taken for granted,

    Has mother at a loss

10

Conspiring with rude intervention,

    Is mans imposed disgrace,

And harmfully seeded intention,

    Grows hard facts of life to face.

11

Air, breathed without strife,

    For more than just enjoyed,

Now a polluted threat to life,

    From profit scans employed.

12

As contaminants one cannot feel

    For every soul aware,

Metastasized lungs never heal,

    Running out of air.

13

And water flowing undrinkable,

    As cataclysmic sin,

Yet worse by far, unthinkable,

    Mother has no twin.

14

From this fate invited illusion

    Is an emptying glass endowed

With sands for a timed illusion,

    For corrections sake allowed.

15

Burdened now by over birth,

    Does she hone some grisly swords

For severance. As our ties to earth

    are cut. Such fragile fetal cords —

16

Were never faithfully connected,

    One sided, and now too late.

For minus lifelines respected,

    We yet procrastinate.

17

Lines major connections,

    Seen as, in tempted fate

applying bad corrections,

    As we overpopulate.

18

Not seeking satisfaction

    She sets the rules exact.

Considering resurrection,

    Calls a "Vanishing species act"

19

No one holds an insurance plan

   For guarantee survival

The late detracted time on hand

    Has mother in denial.

20

So warned, raging waters rise,

    To high's as never seen,

For earth's creations are mother's eyes,

    Covered to redeem.

21

Harsh wails echo, to no avail,

   As evidenced in sin,

Locked upon a comets tail,

    Exasperates her spin.

22

Reconciliation placed,

    For people to emerge

As better humans faced

    Without the usual scourge.

23

For these left as she rebounds,

    From indisputable strife.

Separating the cursing sounds,

    For prayers, to blessing life.

24

Be for mother's sake

    Sees a lessoning greed

For as a future stake,

    It is decreed………….,

H E BRIGHT
12/2008

Who's Path Crosses Whose

Thoughts of pasts determine what lasts,

    If a future is worth being sought.

On extended tours, a traveler explores,

    The life that cruising has brought.

If life beguiles, fate smiles,

    And times provide the years,

With shared love, where the above

    Is laughter with fewer tears.

One easily slips into journeyed trips

    As lifetime's ritual tours,

Have inroad scenes and daunting dreams

    With strange paths crossing yours,

From inner voices, various choices

    See lanes, never endings,

Where curving lines, on many signs,

    Are options recommending

That centerlines, white path designs

    Are narrowed tracks to choose,

In softly shouldered sand, we stand

    When "Whose path crosses who's?"

Crossing fields, of caustic yields,

    Is causing pent amore, as

For how to lose, these stressful views

    Are revealed I the sealed Pandora's.

On some mountain ridges covered bridges,

    People have to pass,

Composting late, is to stimulate

    A special planting's class

As cause to know, what can grow,

    From prestigious air-loom seeds

Is having pure, assumption for,

    How Pilgrims consider deeds

Uplifting goes when a drifting rose,

    Have petals blown about.

As aromas lost, unreinforced

    An essence spreads about.

A good theme when roads turn green,

    In hued skies, jeweled and blue,

Caressing kinds of detour signs,

    Suggesting, "Who finds who?"

For seeds to spawn, is ardor shorn

    Treading crossroads new,

Will a road above have sanctioned love

    Off course? – I haven't got a clue.

On ocean trails, one safety bails

    Before the tides disperse

To seas, the guest of ardor's zest,

    One has never to rehearse.

For year spent, with a love absent

    Feels as hardened steel

In barren time of fewer finds

    Does trophy's crown repent?

The future's repose, flat-lines to suppose,

    Are for times that too, expire.

On the chosen roads, crisscrossing those

    Were reflections we desire.

When treks in springs are precious things,

    As happiness affords

This solemn toast, thanks the host,

    Enjoying trip's rewards.

There is a seasoned, preciously reasoned,

Cruising time, win or lose

Caressings blessed our blessings best,

For "Whose path had crossed who's?"

With Love – H. Ebright
2009

Never Forgetting Ever

in memory of moosh

1997-2009

Suddenly out of the brush

    when summer time was plush

Came a pussycat needing love

Disheveled, alone, most likely lost

    assumed he'd probably been tossed,

Had god sent this friend from above?

He'd been picked with care

    for twelve years did we share

A relationship I'll never forget.

This love i mention, was not my intention

    climbing such heart wrenching steps.

His "so true devotion" deep as an ocean

    is love in unfathomable depths.

But death did up part

    he went with all my heart.

This life, now on hold, i regret.

So It Goes

Cordially toasting, and unwary hosting,

Can invoke disturbing conditions.

Danger increases, as intellect ceases

Controlled by some devil's decisions.

"Live in treasure" he says, "Measure your pleasure"

But advantage, are only illusions.

As a long ladder rope swings, knotted for hope

In escaping his sordid intrusions.

"Sides never denied" says our leading tour guide,

Showing paths in his most insistence.

Where evil grows, entitlement shows,

Considered as corrected resistance.

Living is rough, and in life, quills are tough,
  As are sharp pointed ill guided quirks.
With honest objections, people's corrections
  Use whatever fool for them works.

The nativity sort, who most likely fought
  The lion, used plausible care,
Religiously taught with protection naught,
  Had faith chosen, beyond compare

Life readily chooses values, for losers,
  Dreamers were never meant to gain.
Scrupulous guides know mid crises slides
  As assignments known only for pain

Life's listed billings, wrapped in soft twillings,
  Of temptation's un-ironed twinkles
Spent, as a season denies every reason,
  Outshining each cluster's wrinkles.
Abuses Excuses, Styles denials,

To summarize all living cause,

Alibis alkalize, algaecides, genocides,

All from conflicting bylaws,

Pleasures slip the hard times grip,

Yet decency squeezes through.

Everyone knows those, to dodge the blows,

Will have soft hearts pulsing true.

These novel affairs are lifetime wares,

That will shortly all abrupt,

We're beautifully grown, incarnate prone,

And perhaps just slightly corrupt.

So never fear with the sepulcher near,

As most times without remorse,

Were in gracious light, not one sleepless night,

And our going is time's honored loss.

H EBRIGHT 2009

Commitments

Happiness thrives with contentment

    When love is without despair.

It exposes any resentment

    For just those, unaware

That peace should be consistent

    When dedication is at stake,

And living becomes resistant

    To advantages partners might take.

For being reasonably contented

    Just most of the time,

As a measure represented

    By an omen's enamored sign,

In gauging a partner's warmth tenderly,

Let a conscience provide the right

To glow in the spotlight, splendidly,

And bask in heaven's light,

In whose rays, may come exclusions

To dry tears sadly cried

For some wasted years intrusions,

In perhaps greater loves denied.

Life is when living, overtakes

The pulses watchful sentry,

Who's set a pace and even fakes,

In filling one's horn-of-plenty.

How many beings take a vow,

In the course of the failing mind,

Having been around, are finally now,

Convinced that love did find,

Reality, and having the gumption,

To stand alone, unfurled

Relying on the heavenly assumption

There is love for one in this world.

H E BRIGHT 2009
commitments

One Springs

1

Anxiously feeling the winter's demise,

As creation shines life anew,

Elation glows as winter dies

Knowing springs are coming through.

2

Lasted a season of freezing ways

Excitedly, winter departs,

As badly needed warm sun rays

Stop the dripping eave-spear darts.

3

Having slept most frozen days,

With pent up desires and urges,

Now sharing green in nature's craze

Negotiating merges,

4

As the best ways to warm in cold,

    Frustrates the youth potential,

For those released from winter's hold

    In excitement, is considered sensual.

5

Winter argues, being banished,

    And continues the March wind blowing.

Today in warming the snow almost vanished,

    Preparing an April showing.

6

But for his contriving, springtime arriving

    Leaves respecting life's declarations

For the strong hearts, just surviving

    Have no time for celebrations.

7

Such beneficial vitality processed

    Nature's romantic scenes

I'm respecting conceptions, she confessed,

    Devising new earthly greens.

8

As equally shared life's great forces,

    Push crocus up through snow.

Daffodils bunch, as single sources

    Know it's time to grow.

9

A miracle, as the season changed

    For perpetual precious good

Exists, "As heaven's sake arranged."

    Doing the things one should,

10

All this toasting to springing days

   In an optimistic view,

 Is accepting reason's mystery ways,

   Making special dreams come true.

With love

H. EBRIGHT 2009

A Golden Apple

1

Windstorms drain a farmer's pride

    And he wells with mass emotion.

As nature wraths unjustified,

    For years of toiled devotion

2

    Throughout the night, temper tears

    The fruit from his apple trees,

Each lightening shredded limb bears,

    The brunt of nature's breeze.

3

His cries beyond the pain and yields,

    With summer, all but done,

The storm damaged fruitless fields

    Are gone, gone all but one.

4

And of felled trees sad inspection,

    One blessed is special gender,

Missed the miseries of rejection,

    As a gift from an intender.

5

Now for nature to decide,

    On a pathway lineage tree,

On a fork in branches can provide

    A who goes, or stays serendipity.

6

Before the times have stripped trees tall,

    Before we strap on boots.

Before the rounds of sculptured fall,

    And the cold rejects the roots.

7

Before the times again will lengthen

    Affords the will to sow.

Before the warming sun can strengthen

    Accords, and planters grow.

8

And provide nurturing genes

    For vital procreation,

Finding ways, by any means,

    To natures consummation.

9

And so it found a warmed up place,

    In winds of tender floe,

A precious seed of apple's race

    And a cored up will to grow

10

Determination knows the ways

    This plight needs to unfold

The sun, as yet to bend its rays,

    To deny a seedling's hold.

11

Fewer warm obliging days

    Remain as cold descends,

In fertile ground the lodging stays,

    And the race with time extends-

12

Through winters fall and harsh extremes

    It lasts with prayers of psalms

Sleeps with soft white blanket dreams,

    Of luscious apple farms.

13

Trees of this green spacious ocean

    Endure as growth dictates

His work is perpetual motion,

    As destiny's touch percolates-

14

And directs this grand supervisor,

    The powerful creator of deeds,

The only one formalizer

    Lets apples mature from seeds.

15

He replanted the trees

    From the one that stayed,

And in green seas gentle breeze.

    He's so glad he prayed.

H.E. Bright

1-2009

The Tutor

Intrigue stimulates us golden fools,

    Teaching little ones that about schools.

Starting from scratch, does an egg comes to hatch,

    When a grandparents demonstrate rules.

A gardener tills, a tiny brain fills,

    And a new one yearns to learn.

From scratch teach a baby, and then perhaps maybe,

    With patience, see little minds churn.

Having assumed a pleasurable chore,

    On this so honored wonderful tour,

Arranging word dealings, is strange for young feelings,

    Teaching a young one to explore.

I see an aura, as she grins,

    And view a halo, void of sins.

This aid from my heart is a simple head start.

    So a lifetime of learning begins.

Now groping to choose, and clutching at clues,

    Those one's and two's of learning,

At just past four, she says, "two two's and more",

    And I see tiny etchings burning.

Not all things are fun, for a so tiny one,

    Is jittery, with latent ambition.

With numbers galore, and letters to explore,

    And it is I, who is blessed for tuition.

Her two bright eyes shining are diamonds to mining,

    As she eagerly faces the strain,

And each explanation needs hard concentration.

    So rough shapes a tiny new brain,

An incentive near, is her old sister peer

    Who at nine peaks competitions,

More intellect there, with intelligence to share,

    Perks our little one's thoughtful renditions.

In this world I show, all is new to know,

    As this tiny sponge sops up the void.

When energies calm she finds learning is charm,

    With surprising renditions enjoyed.

Her readings are words memorized,

    As an A B C's book implores,

With lines plagiarized, sentences are vandalized,

    From the pages she mostly adores.

And so this beginner, as one lucky winner

    In a new world, she wonderfully explores,

Is aided persuaded, so young, yet un-jaded,

    With dramas, she patiently endures.

Beginnings are the start, we're all yet a part,

Of learning, it goes on forever,

Comes as an endeavor, for one to be clever,

For help is the least of my heart.

Here in my teaching, instilled in my preaching,

Is spirit with virtue and gains.

That she learns from me, is her destiny to be,

A part of this mortal's remains.

H. EBRIGHT 5/2009

SHOULD POEMS RHYME

1

Ideas forming a central theme

    In simplified thought interactions,

Can rhyme in a poem so one can dream

    Using symmetrical thought satisfactions.

2

Arranged renditions with tenderness, employs

    Beautifully implied contractions.

Rhymes that work, if a poet enjoys,

    Soothing symmetrical abstractions.

3

Tender orations have a voice,

    For blending precious thought

As a sculpture chiseling feels his choice

    In options deftly sought.

4

Imagining waves forming even flow,

Conveying word smoothing rhyme,

Has a writer's brow in an auras glow,

Portraying wisdom's mime.

5

To read a poem of question marks

As other than amusing,

Are conflicts also, like nature's quarks

Get exasperating and confusing.

6

As frustration grips, lips distort

From quoted contradictions

Ringing ears stray firmly taught

Needing rhyme of sweeter renditions.

7

When context lends

    In sweet thought trends

For consensual blends,

    Plasticity mends.

8

A pulsing heartbeat's rhythmic goal

    For smoothing body trauma,

Should beat in synch with mind and soul

    And cure un-rhymes of drama.

9

Exceptionally dear when poems end clear

    Is enjoying the works of a poet.

Too near is sheer fear of thought we hear

    In disillusion, that we often show it.

10

I cannot pose (write) in other than rhyme

    And my work is usually clever

It cannot be offbeat, out of line,

    For my writing is not an endeavor

H. E. Bright
10/2009

CHAPTER 3

Mary – Sick and Passing Over:

2010 - 2012

During this time, Mary's sister Yolanda passed away, leaving her alone without siblings for the first time. She was relying on Harold a bit more. His poems displayed their relationship as it was changing. By 2011, she would be diagnosed with cancer.

Mary was Harold's third wife and was 20 years his junior. Everyone (especially him) assumed she would be there to take care of him until he died. But, like one of his favorite sayings, "Man makes plans, and God laughs" or something like that.

That year, she was diagnosed with pancreatic cancer. She fought it vigorously, valiantly, but in the end, it prevailed and she passed away. Harold had to fend for himself. We tried so very hard to convince him to be nearer to any of us, (Florida, Westchester or Long Island) yet he insisted he was where he wanted to be, which was in Paradise.

Happily Married

1

Like bliss in heaven, being wed at first,

When love and affection can't satisfy thirst,

Has everything new, except time to rehearse,

Blinded by love sonnets soul-searching verse.

2

Happily married, is early in bed,

Safely covered. With false feelings shed

For longer investments, trust seals the wed,

Till uncertainties change thoughts being said.

3

Staying together, upon the bustling side,

Of one, being granted as Satin's pride,

Is one frenzied mate, that tears cannot hide,

In a partner's love, on a fear strained ride.

4

Mates can be hazardous, simply stated.

In stressful matters uncompensated

Prone to marvel less argue ably rated,

Making peace for partners complicated.

5

Scenes of the night so darkened late,

As tensions bite by the parking gate,

Sense the fight in a barking mate

Up tight as an omen's sordid fate.

6

Tensions might in a caustic state,

Cause the plight of steps un-straight,

Then the flight subordinates hate,

For a sure sigh fight for opiate.

7

Neither scores the perfect ten,

    When thirsting lust coerces yen,

And roughness taints a ruffled den,

    Inviting partings version then,

8

Has one to trouble Mate with acorn,

    In living proof of states forlorn,

And vexing has with tongue and horn

    Elusive illusion's sadly borne.

9

Achievements dim when eyes have cried,

    For sarcastic tongues, in those with lies,

And tolerance depends with equal pride,

    When peace will come, as someone tries.

10

A bar to hop, a rail to perch

    The fight for stimulations search

All tested scenes in single's church

    Overlooks coerced besmirch.

11

But what of the love that ruffled piles,

    In flaky tended growing miles,

In reservations harsh denials,

    To equalize the partners riles.

12

To spat and curse, afflict the woe,

    From two, two need a drama show,

Hotly defend their portions blow.

    As when two sides seed, a love to grow.

13

Smoothness is love and doubly just

    When sureness knows that honest trust,

Can doubt away the sordid lust,

    Then 'Never the same twice" a-wedded must

14

The needed pace contents the cause,

    The feel for love cements the pause,

To live as one by spiritual laws,

    Outweighs the slamming bedroom doors.

15

Devotions sparred upon the mate,

    Gently meshed, geared never too late,

Forever feared but best for fate,

    As a true love's destinations date...

16

Now for those wiser and tolerably sure,

    Of years fast passing, leaving less to
    explore,

Till a wish at last breath, is for just one more

    For a happy relationship, or an afterlife
    tour.

H.E.BRIGHT 2009

COMES THE SUNSHINE

This precious season springs, and warms
    The frozen roads and hills,
To thaw from dirty unplowed storms,
    And melt the snow crowned sills.

Times have changed, as age expands
    The days so carefully measured,
To re-arrange living commands
    For existence being treasured.

Bodies, for their needs it seems
    Can recover life, restored
Finding warmth in those directed beams
    Provided as cherished rewards

Intriguing are the paths of reason

    Produced for living strong

Easier said in spring's special season,

    As the winter's glad parting song.

Shine you sun, with your fires warm

    Soothing solutions in crisis

Provide a seasonal port in a storm

    Of rages and inherited vices.

So springs the world, with flags unfurled,

    With life experiencing times,

With the loves of wealth, as the joys of wealth,

    In the presents of spiritual minds

Harold Ebright 4/4/10

ODE FOR RETIREMENT

Half opened eyes on blurry skies
    For another dull day expected.
Life is a drag, when time hits a snag,
    With my living and job connected,

A birdy singing, my clock is ringing,
    Better waken, get to shaken.
Soft was teddy, I leave the beddy,
    Feet find floor and fetch to door.

Got to wash the groggen, fluff the noggin,
    and powder well. (should not smell).
Found, eggs and bacon downed, hasten
    Racing, pacing, times a-wasting.

With crippling busses hard on trusses,

    And walking bumpy, cheap shoes lumpy,

Cabbies hacking, and subways packing,

    For revenue quest, the work I detest,

Too hassling lines, shoving times

    People packing lifts are stacking.

The usual crunch, squashes my lunch,

    I'm here at nine, on time, on a dime.

Coffee and sinker, eyes the blinker,

    Desk's a-winker, they pay the thinker.

For the clock I'm watching, work is blotching

    The gossips mention, boss has tension.

Working jerking, cramped insane

    Computer bane, this job is pain

The his abusing, is very confusing,

    I think of five, in a drinking dive. (amusing)

Must create a plastic shell,

    Bottled well from this drastic hell

An idea sought, oddly thought,

    Perhaps for naught "My soul was bought"

In light house dreams, bluntly speaking

    I'm settled now and seriously thinking,

Of an alien garden, firmly linking,

    Happiness was once a beacon blinking.

To the final hours, when eternity suggests,

    As this troubled soul requires

With promises void, of life's requests,

    Peacefully asleep, as the ground desires

H.E.Bright
7/2010

THE LIGHTHOUSE

As sun rise rays purpose the days
    On another morn for working scorn
To smell the air, for none to share
    For another day, of life's dismay

 Birdies singing, clock a ringing
    Gotta waken, get to shaken.
Soft was the beddie nesteled to teddy
    Feet on floor, find the door.

Wash the groggen, fluff the noggen,
    Powder well, (anti smell)
With eggs n bacon, gotta hasten,
    Brown bag packen, no time for slacken

Cabbies hacken, subways packen

    Don't hesitate, Can't be late.

Crippling buses, hard on trusses

    And shoes lumpy, walking's bumpy

To hasseling lines (shoven times)

    People packen lifts, all stcken

The usual crunch squashed my lunch,

    But arrived at nine on a dime.

Coffee and sinker, desk a winker

    Clock, I'm pushin this jobness coushin

As most deletes are endless sheets,

    And gossips mentions causes tensions.

Racken packen stacken swish

    Worken jerken quirkn tish

Boss a-bashin, time to cash in

    To smile thinking, at five for drinking.

This work for pay is tribulation

    Caused by crass necessity

Another day in speculation

    Fuels the tangs of poverty

Create a-lastic plastic shell

    So bottled well in drastic hell

Has truly wrought this naughtly thought,

    An idea caught, a soul was bought

Of lighthouse dreams (bluntly speaking)

    I share alone with precious thinking

Of an Eden's garden can tightly link,

    Happiness, as just a beacon's blink.

HAROLD E;BRIGHT
2010

RESPECT

1

No body lives the everlasting.

    Only time has a continuous stake

For those justified in passing

    to spread genes for populace sake.

2

 A way to spend the time he lends

    The moments tend the seasons end,

To understand how nature sends

    Arrangements blend with every trend.

3

Once a year the calendar page

    Delivers warmth for frost,

Economy saw the woodsman's rage,

    Fuming for comforts cost -

4

That found his fall of drifted leaves

    That covered his frozen ground,

That blew white snow through barren trees,

    That compacted piles around.

5

Re attached now, new for fluttering,

    Are the leaves, as buds get fed,

With warmed winds passive mutterings

    The end of a freezing dread.

6

But winter argues being banished

    Astride the March winds blowing

Warmer breezes, and snow has vanished

    And warmed up the piles now showing.

7

These are the rearrangement days

    As a light lengthened slow thaw starts

Warming casts the new suns rays

    For the dripping eave spear darts.

8

From snowbound lifeless winter times

    Comes renewed inspiration

As a miracle springs, and rewinds

    On a masterful presentation

9

Of nature choosing floral tides

    To glorify her ways

Of summer, showing garden slides.

    That warm and calm the days,

10

Of the blessings that springs, exceptional

    Is the wonder of truth in life's dream

Expecting the impossible for redemption

    making seasonal greatness, supreme.

11

On scheduled flights a crowded race

    Of snowbirds arrive,

Circle yearly for privileged space

    For a seasoned reason to thrive

15

For he who grants this life to bear,

As mush more, than to conceive,

Is he whose breath we truly share.

Of his gift we wish to receive.

H.E.BRIGHT

2010

WORDS OF WISDOM

1

Nothing lasts forever, quote

    The writers, not to mention,

How clever them that ever wrote

    Of lives without exemption,

2

What they consider realization

    An author's world, might consist

Of coordination in frustration,

    Showing life as it might exist.

3

Parody needs clarity as an iffy evaluation

    Suspects the intellects of spiffy
    communication.

Words assigned as "sties of swine"
pronunciation,

    Are discussing cussing, to define
    enunciation.

4

Engage the rage, of scripted instigations,

    Quotations of insidious morality,

Twisted synapse aggravate preparations

    When kind minds try hospitality,

5

Authors have rights to the blank page

    They alone energized

And the book of life at every stage

    Is open to be plagiarized.

6

Everyone reads and a writer exceeds,

    Having mustered his share of tuition.

Ability exceeds what education decrees,

    And publication can't cause malnutrition.

7

Freed of strain is pen and brain

    So scripted, being sought.

A talent admires, love's need inspires pain

    But happy years can come to naught.

8

For nothing looms when senility dooms,

    With denials as a mind is consumed.

Long past utility, stability entombs

    Cast to stone, is bone un-resumed

9

Left for posterity, wisdom and clarity

    Writings sincere to measure

Reverence for prayer, posterity and charity.

    Incredible are words of treasure.

10

Only through the creation's manipulator

    To provide wisdom for writing's dispersal,

At resourceful connections, the supreme
creator

    Makes teaching, entirely universal

Harold Ebright
1/2011

A CENTER FOR ALL

1

Our creator shows partiality

    Showing human's observation

As all the harshness in reality,

    Is for just consideration.

2

Giving insight to see

    For the choice of convictions

It was decided for true life to be

    Just cause for eased restrictions.

3

As our creation is commanded

    Eternity gets involved

And gets a reasonable brain expanded

    With intellect and resolve.

4

This species centering on originality

    All massive above, subatomic below

Where we contemplate mortality

    As this gifted world bestows.

5

Humanity is in the middle, If anyone cares,

    There to resolve a world of data.

And for balance in the center, as if someone dares,

    To argue this theory of matter.

6

As a center for all this beautiful space,

    Is a creator's master plan

Assured with grace will gently embrace

    The spirituality of man.—

7

For good reason, do intelligent brains

    Consider revelation

As enlightenment, and awareness explains

    Reality is but pure observation.

8

We extract are laws, Divine interventions,

    Is to erase existing sin,

We're pardoned for our worst intentions,

    Of blasphemies held within.

9

Centralizing what the master conceives

    He knows love will contrive

For every gene and he believes

    That spreads in the cosmos, survives.

10

Presented for mankind

    Is love with explanation

Centered for the mind

    Is as heaven's creation.

11

This gift of choice, the makers love

    Designed for human's bliss

On earth, our grant from that above

    Is with blessings and righteousness.

12

A conscience observant intelligent brain,

    Sees where cleaver can be forever,

Has for only karma to explain

    The majesty of creation's endeavor

H.E.BRIGHT   1/ 2011

THE VISITORS

1

Illusion is my solitude

    Intrusion ruins the peace

It takes enormous fortitude

    Where problems never cease

2

Annoyances of many forms

    Have stresses that persist

As rages, qualms and tempest storms

    Create how I exist,

3

Peace is rare in my comfy chair

    Expecting to relax,

As eyes stare at movements there,

    Something is making tracks.

4

Tiny shadows, seeking the narrows

    Creep to a darkened room.

From the kitchen door, hugging the floor

    Is an invasion, and tensions loom

5

They try to decide in a crevice to hide,

    Like spies on a perilous mission,

For them here to abide, housing is denied!

    And best someplace else! I'm wishen!

6

An unrespectable intrusion, of unacceptable profusion,

    Is implored, but not ignored,

Perturbing, disturbing, and unnerving,

    Record this invasion, as abhorred

7

Resigned to race, aligned to face

    The consequence of a chase,

A bug's parade, a crusade charade

    Invades my private space.

8

Have they come here to procreate,

    And take what I possess?

This I don't appreciate.

    So extermination is next, I guess.

9

They are bugs, arrogant thugs

    Crawling in corner dregs

To increase their species ugly, in feces,

    Off springing their buggy eggs

10

They have every right to existence

　　Even with all my resistance

They have every right to be,

　　As long as they don't live with me

11

As creation is divinity

　　Living is genuwinity

Existence is complacently, smug

　　Dying is a certainty.

12

The right to survive, is being alive

　　But only the beginning of sorrows

Life lives when joy forgives,

　　With love for the better tomorrows

**Harold
Ebright 3/3/11**

BE CAUSE

1

The made Creation

    As that to define

As in all expectation

    Of what is Devine

2

Creation as the designs

    For perfection of our minds

And a creator assigns,

    Direction.

3

As receivers of a decree

    Might seek reflection,

For every right to be

    Might need correction.

4

With perfection comes conversion

    Where interpretation of a kind

Could consider perversion,

    As are most inclined

5

So know discretion,

    If that as planned

Shows repression,

    Would disregard the first command

6

To refine the Devine,

    Exchange is implied

There is only heaven sublime

    Changes are denied.

7

Was made for us, and our existence

A creation to conceive in

And acceptance without resistance

Is continuity to believe in

8

So for every sigh, without a "t"

Is how one will come to see

How from nothingness, but for you and me

Is now everything there, so we might
Be-Cause

H.E.Bright
1-2012

A HAPPINESS ALPHABET

Happiness is a:

A   An empty apple sauce tree container

B   A big burly bag of burritos

C   A cautious contented cuddly calico cat

D   A dissolved domestic duties dowry

E   An endeavored extreme episode,
      extricating escape

F   A fabulous feature furthering fame and
      fruition

G   Getting a Golden Globe with Gidget

H   A healthy hopeful happy harlot, (heated)

I   An integral interval of irrefragable intellect

J   A jade jewelry jamboree

K   A kindness for Karma kept King size

L   A loveable useable illustrious latrine

M   A mother's masterful magic, marooned on
      Maui

N   As nature's natural nonsense nefarious,
      nonstop (evil)

O   An unordinary obsession with obscenity

P   A pinup perhaps the perfect paycheck, putt or penis

Q   A quantity of quelled quills and qualms

R   A rarely recaptured rainbow's relief

S   A sequel for a sentimental setting sun

T   A tenderness tangibly taught tightly together

U   An understanding of this unusual universe

V   A vivacious vulgar victory

W   Worthy of worship

X   Exponents of Xmas

Y   Yes – We have bananas

Z   A zilch of all zits

THE SADNESS ALPHABET

SADNESS is a:

A   An appendage appraisal

B   A burst broken beer bottle

C   A confused carnal captivator committing

D   A default of one's designed destiny

E   An evil extortionistical evangelist

F   A frigid frustrated female

G   A grotesque grouchy Gnu

H   A humongous hustling hussy

I   An insulting imposing inquisition

J   A jabbering jackass (jabberwock – L. Carol)

K   A katydid in a kettle calling

L   A loosely lined layette

M   A morbid mutilator's masterpiece

N   A narcissistic naturalist

O   An offensive official officiating

P   A perverse perturbed parish parishioner

Q   A queasy questionable quaff

R   A repentant revelation

S   A shameless sequel to a seduction

T   A termite testing terra-cotta

U   An unclean undergarment unwashed

V   A videotaped vile vixen

W   A wall-street washout warning

X   An exotic X ray

Y   A Yin and Yang Yoke

Z   A zygote zapped

HAROLD EBRIGHT
3/8/12

What's It All About

A Creator designed for the human mind,

    And so we're given direction

As in all expectation creation is Divine,

    in everyway, shape, and form, perfection.

Shortened, to be better perceived,

Creation assigned

    for humans, direction.

A creator designed, for humans,

    - Perfection.

What was made to believe in, is for our existence

    A creation to conceive in, without resistance, was planned

Best with discretion, for better expression,

    Is to acknowledge his first command.

That says simply,

A creator assigned

    For the human, direction

The creation thus, as designed

    As "Perfection"

As is with every right to be,

    Should respect correction.

We receivers of decree

    Need protection

And as if in this made creation

    We might define,

 For greater expectation

    For that which is Divine

H e bright 5/20/12

We're gifted with special guides that participate

 In giving us a share of creation to live in.

We're all born to procreate, procrastinate, and deteriorate

 As death promises the final judgments be given...

THE REAL STRING THEORY

Shuffle a deck and a card is selected

 With results of fate often changed

Would something control things neglected,

 And our course through life rearranged.

2

We live cruising a pre-charted tour

 Crisscrossing seas, unexpected

Somehow predetermined and not bartered for,

 As we sail on a course pre-selected.

3

Always hopeful calm waters prevail

    With an outcome somehow preplanned.

Being arranged, by them, where and why we sail

    Have the waves and tidings at their command.

4

A battle for existence has every bout

    Getting wrestled from ominous things.

Omens derive signs without doubt

    Something is pulling our strings.

5

Assisting minds not sure

    Correcting fraudulent schemes

Resisting thoughts not pure,

    And by the strangest of means

6

At the beginning, when human arrived

    Nothing was denied

But to aid in their survival,

    Better decisions were supplied

7

Life is seas of foam with high surfs galore

    So for calmer waters bound.

Are shown much better ways to endure

    For riches, bays, and solid ground

8

Maybe angels with auras over their heads

    Appear with glowing rings

Saints, perhaps preparing our beds

    Were they guides pulling our strings?

9

Would be nice to have command

    If a future was to persevere

But that goodness we couldn't understand

    Kept showing us how to steer.

10

So blessed is he, or maybe she

    That has directed all our travels

And saw our strings so weak to be

    Everlasting, as life unravels.

11

One exists when life resist

    Needing all that help can gather

Just knowing a course is not at a loss

    Is the kind of life I'd rather.

H.E.BRIGHT
8/10/12

MARY

YOU'RE GONE, I'M NOT

    I GRIEVE, BUT HAVE NOT FORGOT

THE LOVE WE HADE AN AWFUL LOT-

    THAT NOW FILLS TO BRIM, YOUR
    ASHES POT.

KNOWING LONELYNESS, NOW AS ONE,

    AS LOSS AMOUNTS, ACCOUNTS TO
    NONE

THIS PAIR SO CLIEVED, THE BOND
UNDONE

    AN OPPRESSIVE WEIGHT, BLOCKS
    THE SUN-

ON SHATTERED PIECES, THE BROKEN
MOLD

    OF WHAT HAD BEEN, IS NOW ON
    HOLD

A PAIR OF WINNERS THAT OF GOLD,

    IS NOW THE PAST, THE PAGES FOLD.

AND OBSCURE THE PATH OF WISHES LED

TO WORDS OF WISDOM, HOPES THAT
SAID,

"NOBODY'S PERFECT" SOME TO DREAD,

ALONE AND SAD NOW, AS AN EMPTY
BED

IF WE TO WALK WITH FRIEND GALORE,

COULD STAY OUR TIMES, AS WE
EXPLORE

WOULD WATCH OUR BACKS, FOR EVER
SURE,

FOR ALL THE SADDNESS WE ENDOUR

LIFE GOES ON, AND ON FOREVER,

IT CANNOT END FOR THE SOUL'S
ENDOUVER,

FOR OUR BODIES HERE AS PROOF SO
CLEAVER

OF AN ENERGY FORCE THAT EXPIRES,
NEVER

HAROLD EBRIGHT
9/7/12

MARY'S GONE

To know loneliness, now as one

    As loss accounts, amounts to none.

Our pair so parted, a bond undone,

    As an oppressive shadow blocks the sun-

On shattered pieces of a broken mold,

    For what had been, is now on hold

We paired as winners, that of gold,

    Is now the past, and the pages fold.

You're gone, I'm not

    I grieve with rage and forgot

The love we had, an awful lot,

    As tears fill to the brim, your ashes pot.

And obscure a path of wishes that led

    From your words of wisdom, hopes that said

No one's forever, some to dread,

    Are alone and sad now, as an empty bed.

To walk with friends in warmth, and share

    Who watch our backs, and be aware

If all the sadness we could bear

    To stay our time, Life is not fair!

But it goes on, and on forever,

    It cannot end the Soul's endeavor,

For our bodies here, as proof so cleaver,

    Of an energy force that expires, -Never.

H. EBRIGHT
9/23/12

CHAPTER 4

What Was –
Paradise, or,
Assisted Living:

2013

What is Assisted Living? A few months after Mary passed away, Harold had pneumonia. Luckily (because of Kim's foresight) he was transported to a hospital in Westchester, where he received really, really good care. We were also able to visit him more frequently, not being over 100 miles away. He was in the hospital almost two months. As he was very weak and not really able to care for himself (especially if he were two states away from anyone and alone) he visited several independent and assisted living facilities in Westchester. After finding one we thought he said he liked, Kim spent tremendous amount of time moving his things and buying sufficient amounts to make this his nearby home.

Alas, he did get better, and maybe because he was not able to drive, or he didn't really know the area, or he didn't have a garden to take care of, he grew very bored. There is an increase in the number of poems during this time. At some point he decided it was time to go home to his paradise – by having a friend come and get him and trying to not let us know he was making his escape. We tried to stop him from going to a place far away, with no help and a big, big house, but he could not be deterred.

The compromise was to look into independent homes near his home, which he did ultimately find and move to. The poems of this period have, at least to me, a bit of a sarcastic twist. This is the time he staged his own "coo" to return to his paradise, the home in Pennsylvania.

THE HEN HOUSE

There was, in a henhouse, chickens laying,

    Happily content and brimming,

Boas, feathers flying , no denying

    These were chickens with all the trimmings.

Twelve resided, nested and assured,

    That each section had layers aboard

Nesters came, a price procured

    To the chickens delight in accord—

With brooding times, and ruffles and toil,

    Lest the labor of love cracks a shell,

Happiness assures other moments will spoil,

    And smoothness has splinters too swell.

So smoothly they vested money that itched

   Stashed as a precious nest egg

When a safe he smelled, his cunning nose
twitched

   Found the hen house, a professional YEGG

Came not for chicken

   But to steal her nest box,

Madams eggs for picken,

   Came Whily the fox.

He wooed all the chickens questioning slyly

   Charm he emitted like gold

Where the bounty she kept, prodded Whily,

   As his real purpose here, can unfold-

Such real easy Pickens, assured of his luck

   Told of a safe in madam's abode

Brazen and pluck, he slithered and snuck

   to the nested egg stash. Now just the code.

The safe was too easy, but a noise made him
queasy,

    Behind him twelve chicks in a snit

They found his questions were sneaky
suggestions

    For a purpose not exactly legit.

With his hands on the dial, he came up for trial

    Twelve chicks will never be plucked

Madam egged them on, as Whily's sad qualm

    Getting caught in the act, got him
shucked—

Like an ear of corn

    Had its kernels detached

Whily ran, forlorn,

    With his manhood snatched

H EBRIGHT
1/15/13.

WHAT'S IN A DREAM

The phone rings and I get teed
>   It's four A M, I double check,
>   If the phone had other parts, I'd need
>   To gladly wring its neck—

"Hello, Hello" to empty space.
>   No answer coming through.
>   I have caller I D, and can easily trace.
>   So now what do I do?

For my aggravation and pulse rate
>   I wait, impatiently.
>   At 4:AM, what would compensate,
>   For an interrupted dream's intensity

"Hello again" to an open line where,

    When someone rustles the phone.

I sense tears dripping, and feel hurt and despair

    In the sweetness of her troubled tone.

    I seldom recall dreams when awake

    And rarely does one measure up,

Only sometimes, tenderness lingers to make

    A real overflowing pleasure cup.

Still four A M, and the night can wait

    To restore my sensuous dream,

Sleep has paused to fabricate

    More sentimental themes,

Back to the phone, If ever a voice

    Has the sound, of an angel's fears

Crying for help that obliterates my choice,

    As my mind visions warm troubled tears,

I pick up a cold cradled phone to wonder,

Had I hung it up in disbelief?

When I look for a call back number,

The I D is blank, piercing my grief.

For awhile so concerned, now I'm beaming

It finally crosses my mind.

I had dreamt is a dream, I was dreaming.

But I checked the I D, one more time.

I've never encountered a voice this pure,

For it was love at "first sound"

And as fate would have it, there is no cure.

This one must be found.

Her voice had, when the phone rings now,

A reminder, so beautifully pure,

What remains of passion, in that which we vow

Are those things worth living for.

H E BRIGHT, 2/24/2013
like Applesauce

PERMISSON FOR REMISSION

Dawn thaws the icy dew

    And the sun melts the night

Drains the chill from a lucky few

    As a street dweller's amenable right

Surviving in the city is tough enough

    Searching a path for summer

Just existing is rough enough

    For this life anywhere, is a bummer

With latent dreams of silver spoons

    And fascinating care,

They emerge from putrescent rooms

    Stealing pushcart vender's wear

Malicious, as a doctor's fee

    Exposing patient's plight

Life as indiscriminate, for you and me,

    We are as commodities, out of sight

When symbiotic relations cleverly account

    For being satisfied, coldly coerced

A hoarder is in horror, with any amount

    Of his treasures being dispersed.

We're luckily the sum of many parted

    A perfect product, nearly finished

Dating accounts from when birth started

    Could end abruptly and blemished.

Years behind us haven't changed

    What luck and fate could call

The bleeding heart, so estranged

    For just being here at all

Could have been us on the street

  Struggling and compromised

From that which gave life the beat

  Of the pulse, that we realized

And It's called liven

  Not exactly for everyone

 Balancing out what we were given,

  Punctuates what is done

And so a balance, as it goes

  For just so long, as

Intelligence and indifference shows

  In everything, that everyone has.

So for what could be, or might have been

  And who says for right or wrong

The die, cast as goodness or sin

  Is ringing, searching the final song

H EBRIGHT 2/28/13

WHEELCHAIR MARATHRON

Wise and tempered having lived this long

Seeing reality, as having been there

Traveled the rails and sang every song

For perception is being aware.

Then following a crude compulsion

And never taking a chance

That might becomes emotion

Has allowed leveraging for circumstance.

Says a wise old one of eighty,

Looking for booking a date.

"I'm young and I've sung for the lady,

Some one cooking, watching our weight

The choice of a partner is crucial

    For those who partake of the booze,

Making selections of wines, mutual,

    Is a factor in how one can choose—-

A drinking buddy with potential

    Not a sot or a broken down crutch.

One with preferences essential,

    To good gravies and wines, in our hutch.

At this age not much makes us happy

    To share drunken stupors and fuss

With two maybe more, for this pappy,

    Is a dirty old man with a truss.

The sum total of experience is reality,

    Where perception is action as such

A reaction again, just a malady

    When only visions become the real touch.

H E BRIGHT 3/ 3/ 13

SPRING'S AHEAD

This setting is yearly by ritual

    For a shifting copious season (much)

    From winter come attitudes spiritual

    As encounters are given to reason

    A mist shrouded white hilly landscape

    Sees the rising sun waking the dawn

    Some suns shine brighter, like a keepsake

    But this one embraces the forlorn.

You have to know where to look

    For that shining lights gracious reward

    Is not just east, as accorded the book,

    But for entitlements being restored

It's cold, yet spring rearranges

    Pushing crocus up, while still snowing,

That baffles the cold white strangeness

    But warms the appetite for spring sowing

A time to hasten the winter's departure

    To melt icicle spears from the eves

To warm the hearth with rapture

    And prompt the season He conceives

Bringing once a year

    As natures decree,

 Spring comes without fear

    And loves you and me

H E Bright
3/13/13

WHEN A TIME WAS THEN

1

Chimes in a clock are voices

    Frozen, deep in years of rime

Preserving in life, times and choices

    Saying it all in rhyme,

2

Tick-tocks mimic pantomime

    Expressing a beating heart

Questioning, questioning for the sign

    That says years can tenderly part —-

3

The pasts are the signs, irretrievable

    Of the oh-so virtuous things

As the arrows pointing ahead, unbelievable

    Now an older vantage brings—

4

An age of sacred patronage

    For our lot to multiply

With a slightly liberal leverage

    As in masses to sanctify

5

Only He selecting a sign

    Decided who is involved

For a peaceful world of space and time

    Is how things get resolved ——

6

For that to be, was mostly requested

    To preserve our precious finds

Needing intuition invested

    Expecting greater kinds.

7

Only in a universe of friend and foe

    Do answers come before questions

New are we that cannot know,

    His decisions stem from suggestions

8

Time and futures become the past

    At the closing blink of an eye

Neither so vast, or what might last

    For the middle is when we die.

9

So if you wind a clock too tight

    Oblivious of tomorrow,

Tension springing from narrowed sight

    Will manifest in sorrow

11

The clock that just keeps ticking along

Ages all, with every a tock

Arranges lives in a tick-tock song

Arranging all on this rock

H E BRIGHT
3/23/13

COMFORT LIES BEHELD

Talk to the sky to know that fate

    Does weave the perfect mold

A shape for who, a comfort mate

    Might not strip your gold.

Arts of deception have different rules,

    Pairs, no exception believe in love

As they who lie on piano stools

    Might yet enjoy the sky above

For that as a partner ironed and hemmed,

    Could coddle as one might say

With satisfaction, as something to extend

    And the ease of mind to lay

Besides the nightly neediness

Of pleasure ageing grays

Supplies a time of tenderness

So lacking all the days

If comforts are in measures

For one to simply scale,

With gifted tufts and pleasures

As was sorted from a sale

Like pillars of the soul within

Your cannons ease the sores

Releasing all un-covered sin

Prepared as love assures

And lush requires, to bade desires

For your plush beneath the head

So nestled softly for ones attires

Is for love of a warm precious BED

4/4/13   H.E bright

(NOW REREAD)

COULD YOU BELIEVE

To live on this pile of ups and downs,

    With decisions for existence to enhance

The highs and woes of un-scaled mounds,

    That evoke strange circumstance

On his rock of pits and falls

    Events are usually dramas

People emerging from their stalls

    Encounter the weirdest of traumas

Found one sock the other day,

    The mate got lost, I suggest

It could have walked and gone astray,

    Or maybe it just regressed

Weird stuff occurs when least expected,

Occurrence one couldn't accept

Sometimes with clues hastily rejected

As the signs you shouldn't neglect

While shopping, most shelves are stacked

And a paradox comes, "eggs in a box"

Softly packed, why is one always cracked?

Perhaps by that elusive lost socks

I unlocked the car the night before

And now keys have become hidden

An impossibly possessed car door

Has locked by itself, I'm not kidden

Lost keys play "Tag" a children's game

Even before needing locks

Without its mate, is not the same

As when looking for wayward socks

Attached to the keys, an alarm device

Sends a signal to rule out guessing

Makes finding wayward keys easy and nice

But now lost is the button for pressing.

For sanity at any price

As in the mind of a dreamer who requests,

Perhaps with a friendly poltergeist,

Being helped out with advice he suggests

Recalling memorable themes

Serene, abstract or raging,

For life to fulfill all your dreams

But wisdom, is the price paid for aging

Should senility come, without rhyme or reason,

Sneaking upstairs, like a blanketing fog

Committing the mind's loyalty to treason,

Turning reasoning into smog

With things forgotten, you can't remember

Write them down as little quotes

State, "January always follows December"

By then up to your knees in little notes

So if you worry and fret for tomorrow

Losing so much of today

Making up time, that you will have to borrow,

Shortens your time to play

H.Ebright
4/15/13

For M

A TRIBUTE TO MOTHER

A tribute to our gifted mother

    One so special, as the only one

For there could never be another

    As she orbits the sun

And somewhere under the rainbow's way

    Is so much awe to be respected

Us and animals and birds of prey,

    Those are all as nature suggested.

Beneath that arc, mother's private park

    Is for good, and bad, and between

Some make it, some take it, while others embark

    On this ark, each with a separate dream

We've been recycled on this planet home

    To call this ball our sacred mother

She's earth, and mirth, worth every stone

    As this is all there is, no other.

She bears the fawn creates the dawn

    Our universal doe

To try to leave, is to deceive the dawn

    When there ain't no place to go

Never mind how you believe

    In sizes she's very small

The one true love had to conceive

    As the mother of us all

The mother of us all.

Harold Ebright
4/26/13

ACCEPTANCE

Acceptance is strong, if you belong

On the road of a "Two way street"

Happily strong, when nothing wrong,

Might decide "one way" who'll you'll meet.

Acceptance of love, as the two ways, above

Can design for the self, safe protection

If at the end of the street, if rejection you meet,

Might need an optimal U turn, for reflection,

Nothing is truer than death on a skewer.

Testing adventures un-fulfilled,

Sweetly tasting love, might have found fewer,

Of that which should have been grilled.

And redemptions deliver intentions, chivalrous

Acceptance begins with you

As many a soul in pursuit of a goal

Could be accepted or rejected, but who

Rejection and rages, so oft times contagious,

And exacting a connection to karma

Is how to find peace, Life is outrageous.

The sky is not falling, alarma

Reflectors so often acceptors

Know of good streets, they say

Unknown for yourself, shrewd rejecter's

Often change signs along the way.

Your acceptance of the mirror's golden image

You found pleasing, and not really bad

Knows when YOU best need privilege

And is the best friend you've ever had.

5/16/13
HAROLD EBRIGHT

TO SEE OR NOT TO SEE

Ever so nice, alive and well now

    With many ends yet to tie

So feared then, at the gates of hell, how

    So sick, afraid I might NOT die.

With walking phenomena you opened my door

    And cut like a side of beef

Reestablished a lung to cure

    From a tainted bodies grief

Defying dying, denying to go

    Needing an option in choosing

If death be surrender, Don't let it be slow

    Rather painless and casual and amusing.

Being assessed at death's door,

    By that which takes of the living

Ailing and sickened, needing a cure

    By you doctors of miracles giving

Had death's door closed, restricting light

    On a sickened defeated will,

So beckoned, as too the darkest of night

    Being pushed across the sill.

One only stays for his numbered days

    As mortality is life's divisions

With time so short for a life to abort,

    Come not from our decisions

So now alive, and well again,

    And biding my way

Still breathing, is when

    I can live for another stay.

H Ebright
8/30/13

VISIT A DOCTOR

1

A patient of age, facing his rage

    Unravels his time with fears

As wrinkled old bindings, shed their windings

    He is praying perhaps, for more years.

2

With so many knots left untied,

    At the end of life, unwell

He is fearing, that for all he tried

    Was like standing at the gates of hell.

3

Now with hours wasted and his patience frayed

    In a Doctor's office, his bottom is numb,

Awaiting attention, insurance paid,

    Much disturbed, (Doctor's late) when in he comes!

4

His temper churns, anxiety burns,

   So vulnerable and unaware

Would he address all his concerns?

   And could he really care?

5

"Sorry I've kept you" He says, cautiously snide,

   Seeing one cranky and terse,

If needing a doctor means, clinically tried,

   Could these conditions reverse?

6

Age created ongoing rushes,

   Established as aches and pains.

Like water twisting down a toilet's flushes

   It can pressure, flow in the veins

7

Now asking "Why age has deflated

   This someone trying to share",.

Life's tribulations, trials all debated

   "Indulge me, if you care"

8

"Please help me Doc", If how sick I am,

    I might never be the same,

And is my precious medical plan

    Just more paper down the drain

9

If clumps of molding clay

    Can accentuate an artist's castings,

Can your curing hands show the way

    My future might be lasting

10

Here is an old one tired, rapt and drawn

    Sculptured, hurting and devout,

When I see that expression of scorn,

    In your eyes, Doc, I'm seeing doubt

11

Don't badger me if I can't reply

    To your questions, right away,

I'm embarrassed drooling, and can't rely

    As old senses gone astray

12

If this be an intrusion, on your time,

    And your best can't make me well,

If my cure is an illusion, without a good sign,

    I'll not fear the final bell!

13

I see a door standing ajar,

    Closing, against my will,

Shoving me, having come this far,

    Forcing me across the sill

14

And as my final gasp might suggest

    As my lights dim with despair,

That I might have a last request,

    And be given one more breath of air.

15

Having existed all these years,

    Pride swelled, survived my peers

Having never drowned in hardship tears

    And now can leave, without fears

16

Knowing all along, nothing lasts forever

    So as a courtesy, I can say

What counted most for all endeavor,

    Was having love, and loved along the way.

17

Thank you doctor, how you let me see

    Though rarely did we ever agree,

That the ways of existence are rarely free,

    So bless you guys, how let us be

H EBRIGHT

9/11/13

For all docs of good faith.

OUR CHEF'S SUCCESS

Our chef for many hungry cravings,

    Those who appreciate what cooks

Savors his flavors with ravings

    For succulence, from gastronomical books

His cooking gets attention,

    For the meals that he chooses

Are all at best, not to mention

    Were never known for residue.

He says "Nothing is truer than death on a skewer

    Cooking as my work can suggest,

Hosting, roasting and toasting is truer

    Than the zest of culinary's best"

Tasters, not wasters, enjoy the clatters

    Of reality when, what to pursue

 Are overflowed platters, as what really matters,

    Not to be considered eschew

From suppliers providers, these deciders,

   Assure nothing comes from the zoo,

At most is this menu, hosting this venue,

   Catering to all special, who-

 Are slurping, burping so easily qualmed

   So sated, not expecting repression,

The food alarmed, cannot disarmed,

   They can fluctuate as natural expression

Happiness can come in spastic forms

   And cooking can vary with success

Sometimes arrives as drastic norms,

   Our cookie can now regress.

H. Ebright
9/19/13

STRING THEORY VERSION TWO

From a shuffled deck, a card is selected,

Not only through fate can this changed,

Something else in control, of what is rejected,

And a course through life rearranged.

Consider fate as a charted tour

Crisscrossing seas, unselected

Predetermined as un-bartered for

On a course, varied and unexpected

Ever hopeful that calmness will prevail

For every outcome planned,

But something other, determines how we sail

With the swells at their command

Thoughts get assorted,

    Nothing as it seems

Minds can get distorted.

      Read on these poetic themes.

Existence is living with every bout,

    In a battle from perilous things,

Where omens contrive, as signs without doubt,

    SOMETHING IS PULLING OUR
STRINGS.

There was nothing denied

    At the beginning of human arrival

There better decisions were supplied

    By them who aided our survival

They had Auras over their heads

    That appeared as glowing rings

Saints, perhaps preparing our beds,

    Guides in pulling our strings

Toward placid surfs, firmer shores galore

Toward fertile solid ground

Shown as a better course to explore

For richer paths be found

So for our future to persevere

We were never in command

That course drawn then, was how to steer

With so much more to understand

So bless the he, maybe she

That has guided all our cruising,

Sees our strings that as yet, can't nbe

Left without support when losing.

H EBRIGHT
9/23/13

THE TUCKERER

1

She is one of virtue, one to nurture,

    To stimulate a world of dreams

And heal the sprains and strains of a searcher

    With decisions for troublesome themes

2

When life gets stressed, and very compressed

    She fabricates to console,

This is where she calmly suggests

    That happiness might yet unfold.

3

In worn out woolies, mostly in tatters

    These pajama seams of fuzz

She assails dreams, avails what matters

    This is what a Tucker-inner does.

4

Dreaming is for lives endeavor

    In sleep one might conspire

To adjust for contentment, wherever

    She is there for the greater desire

5

The best tucker-inners can arrange positions

    To placate things denied

Assuring those with lost ambitions

    With help as, they decide

6

A good tuck mends the bluest eyes

    When slumber extends to realize

That sadness provokes the truest lies

    To live as the life of a sad disguise

7

Good sleep can pacify sequels

    Comforts deeply for precious goals

And with psalms to keep prayers as equals

    At the best for all wary souls

8

But sooner or later, we all must wake

    And bring it all in focus

The tucker-inner is just here to make

    Of this world, a Hocus-Pocus

H EBRIGHT,

10/1

PLANTING LOVE

1

A strange relationship was in store

    With a plant I found, (Stories true)

Discarded, so parted, wilted and tore,

    Nurtured by me for years, it grew.

2

In a bright sunny corner, it was endowed

    With privileges for a happy existence,

Thus it gave much more than was allowed,

    In spirit and with persistence

3

Fifty years growing now, it has exhibited

    A resurrected gracious splendor,

Knowing contentment is not prohibited

    When accepting another's gender.

4

All too suddenly, her leaves are showing pain

    I had brought in a tiny young rival

So much for purity, jealousy's strain

    Is an envious green side, for survival.

5

Could a houseplant show indifference?

    Having to give up living space,

Not feeling the security of signiffience

    For each stem, every leaf to embrace

6

For a growing plant without references

    Shallow rooted to specify,

Her entitlement for preferences

    As is for species to modify.

7

"It's only a house plant" someone insists

    And so odd to have feelings on view,

Showing strain when emotion persists

    Now sagging, as her leaves turn blue

8

I have a she-plant, with gratis amiss

    Showing temperament, rousting gender

Feminine is beautiful, but flora with stress

    Is allowed, for us remember-

9

We, the "Yes men" for opportunity

    Would sanctify the loom,

All woven for tranquility

    Should complement the gloom

10

Simplistic is realistic "don't offend."

  Bound by this simple solution,

 We three planted together, to pacify each end,

    Finding this restful resolution.

11

How weird is it to love a plant,

   No stranger than the danger one decrees

Ignoring all reasons saying, "we can't,

     Knowing passion acts on impossibilities

12

Beautifully, she'd never says a word

  In allowing our strange realization

To know how the other is being heard,

  Has keep us growing in anticipation.

H EBRIGHT
10/10/13

EXISTENCE

Existence simply should be respected,

But is not so simple, as expected

To have a purpose, not neglected

And acknowledge creation to be protected.

Why we exist, as opposed to not,

With intelligent eyes to question our lot

As for every season we forget

The very reason we beget.

And for our purpose here observing

Bred with DNA, conserving,

Acknowledges all as so un-nerving

Asking the reason, for our deserving.

For an aspect of our presence

Subjective and selective requires

In observation total essence,

Other than for mortal desires

We alone for interpretation

    With intellectual intelligent persistence

 Act upon our visualization,

    When here only is virtual existence.

It is from people and human observation,

    The acknowledgement of all being true

With our necessity for preservation

    To bring it all in view

If our existence needs explanation,

    Our being here brings sanity,

To an enormous beautiful creation,

    That is nothing, without humanity.

For without US nothing exists.

H EBRIGHT 11/20/13

CHAPTER 5

He's Home –
Paradise PA, or
Thereabouts:
2014

Once he returned to Pennsylvania, Dad found a wonderful independent housing community attached to an assisted living facility where he was able to live in an independent two-bedroom apartment, with its own washer/dryer and two bathrooms.

He was happy – but he was alone. His quest was to find wife #4 so there would be someone to take care of him. But this was Harold, and he had his requirements, first being she should be young, like 55 or 60 years old or younger. And as you can imagine, there are not a lot of women who fit that requirement in PA, who would be looking for an 85 year-young man. As some of the poems attest, it was a difficult search.

Although I know he was lonely, he wanted us to be there for him, and I believe it was a happy time. As he said to me, he was happy to be slowing down. He had never said anything like that to me before.

It seems to me that the poems during this period were a bit more cohesive, perhaps more thought process involved as a result of him having fewer other things to do. He was back home, in his paradise.

PLUCKING TIME

A Deacon of a church got busted,

    Him, staunch as a crown and regal

For a stake in nature he trusted

    Kept everything nice and legal.

Wondered where all the women have gone

    Young chickens, that danced and carried on,

Now this ain't no tale, bout no farm,

    His wanting a chickee, could sound no
alarm.

At a nighttime ball, he found someone new,

    She was tipping a barrel till it drained

He do-si-doed her till light came through

    And preened her feathers, never ashamed.

Here found one to feather his nest,

    Squattely and round, sound at best,

A little top heavy, but nicely compressed,

    Without exception, an ample chest

They danced and spun, uncontrolled

    Never figured what could happen,

Story here to the face, behold,

    Bodies should ever be slappen.

Was it purposefully, a shot to the head?

    As in his nightmare's dream,

At most, an enchanted slap instead,

    Left him agog to beam.

Wacked out once, was all it took

    From a girl so well endowed,

Getting him busted, like a schnook,

    Made him nervously proud.

Happiness for this egg man preacher (To say)

Feathering a nest he saught

As never a "Leg man creacher," (O Lay)

Now enjoying what nature has brought

So to wend ill-conceived and end happy

Does nature at best, compose,

With twice the support for this chappy,

Has surplus, now to compose

H Ebright 1//14

Apple sauce

A-WAY

A-way for this broken one

    To relate, and share

Growing old, is this spoken one

    Knowing roads to despair,

A-Way so spent in life, needed

    A wonderers lust to earn

The soul's lost path that proceeded,

    For that road, of no return,

No guiding posts, no shining stake

    No lanes of tidy pebbled flakes

To appease the heads of crafty fakes

    No ease to burdens, for goodness sakes

A-Way so cast, as fables lost,

    Past exits fast, un labeled, crossed

GPS cast in-abled, tossed

    Time vast unstable, at terrible cost

A-Way to contemplate

And question to believe

A suggested way to tolerate

And emulate, to deceive

Sought the way posted magically

Fought aging, most did prone

Wrought pyres hosted tragically

Caught ashes, of roasted bone

Life's a trip and as the road bends,

No seconds to skip, in time for amends

A sturdy grip on life contends,

As a trip for blessings, before life descends

HEBRIGHT

for applesauce 1/11/14

SPRING TIMES SO WELL

Every year on a given date,

    Nature springs her surprise

Sheds snow and cold to capitulate

    Exactly for winter's demise,

She brings on a "Marching lion"

    To triumph, purging the thaw.

Spring is urging the lamb, try-en

    To strengthen the days before –

Confronting a sun drawing nearer

    Springing a time to unfreeze

The day is changing, much clearer

    Rearranging, and warming the breeze

To minus just one winters day

Can feel slightly younger

Spring brightens, a better way

To trust in the craze of wonder

Time remolds, getting stronger

Spring unfolds rays of gold

Daylight to behold much longer,

The warming controls the cold.

For fortunate beings courageously sought

Caressed by nature's rules,

Saw ignorance, contagiously caught,

From over-stressed wintering fools

For only with insight can we observe,

That all of Nature must be preserved

From each Springing season to conserve

This gift of life, can be deserved

H Ebright
1/20/14
For A S

SON OF A WITCH

A frozen "Witch of the north" Mother,

From an Artic nursery,

Bore a son, like no other

And for all eternity,

2

Called "Old man winter" It was told,

And so was formed an arrogant, mold

Saw of his majesty uncontrolled,

All of winter's travesty, unfold

3

For those so nerved by dangerous games,

On icy roads, and who to blame

On frosted swerves, curved by names

Given for inexperienced driver's shame

4

He instigates, flickering the light

    And gives it all a reason,

For aggravation, hate and spite,

    As he blows away the season

5

Then once in a year, this winter guy

    With frost and cold as staples,

Is said to make the snowman cry,

    Where tears drip from the maples

6

January thaws, some freezing nights

    Sending February, as the way

He procrastination for winter's rights,

    But has forced a March, here to stay.

7

 Spring, springing, has come alive,

    Flaunting his cold suggestion,

Forces the winter to take a dive,

    So amazed by Nature's progression

8

Sprung is nature without permission,

    For April has but one condition

A "Son of a witch" without remission

    Showers on warmth, as his perdition

        —- **H.Ebright   1/25/14   -apls-**

THE YEARS END

One only stays, till his numbered days,

 Have parted, ending a lifetime

Exacting decisions, to reverse ways

 Rejecting unwanted strife time

One can only say of his numbered days

 To recount the least crucial sad ones,

For better conditions, to repent bad renditions,

 May select to accept the glad ones.

Who walks that way

 To pan for gold,

Might treasure each day,

 And earn when to fold.

Happiness, will equalize wrath,

    To neutralize stress and tensions

Could add years on the path,

    Of life's joyful extensions ——

Can make time stretch, wearable,

    If rehearsals insure

To cloak strife, as bearable

    So for peace to endure, (furthermore)

Not easily found on cumbered trails,

    As life ends, ages sad and frail

Having to season times of sad tales,

    Would have kicked the bucket,
    (The preverbal pail)

Demise comes as no surprise,

    But unaccepted when out of sight.

Just don't close your eyes at night,

    All too apathetic to realize

Don't know why I've come to be

    I only know I had to

Grown has shown the family tree

    Needed courage to see it through

—- H Ebright 1/29/14

PERHAPS

So odd on this pile of fertile ground
  Hallowed by our weird existence
Just conceiving, and staying alive
  Shows fortitude and persistence

2

As this round rock, pits and falls
  Contribute to an illusion,
People falls, and shopping malls,
  All act to spark confusion

3

Found one sock the other day,
  Lost was its mate, on the run
It began to fray and went astray,
  To find where it was spun.

4

Strangeness always happens unexpected

    Like that, difficult to accept

With signs connected, badly neglected

    From the minds with no respect

5

Shopping will find shelves neatly stacked,

    Except for twelve eggs in a box,

One is always stuck, slightly cracked,

    Like a poet, writing about socks

6

Locked up the car, and was very confused

    When keys walk, or get hidden

An auto possessed has me stressed and abused,

    It had locked itself, I'm not kidden

7

Bought for my keys, an alarm device
    Beeps to rule out guessing,
  Equals the price by being precise,
    Except lost is the button for pressing

8

Might senility come without reason,
    Sneaking upstairs for confusion
Changing a mind's loyalty to treason
    To make reasoning just an illusion

9

A cure for the cobwebs blurring the air
    With a guarantied outcome so nice
Can cause the laws to being fair,
    And when to stifle a poltergeist —

10

That brought nightmarish dreams

    And unnecessary raging,

Said as part of stranger themes

    To make wisdom the price for aging

11

No matter what lives resolve

    We're tied to an umbilical mother

With no other place except here to evolve,

    For there just isn't another

H EBRIGHT 2/22/14

AWESOME

Could AWE be the bright reflections

    Of pleasures fought for and won,

Perhaps for soul inspections

    Enjoying that said and done

2

A cause for accepting rejections we

    Might pause in AWE, on bended knee

For answers, perhaps corrections to see,

    And marvel in all this majesty

3

Would AWE be with protections,

    On from the nursery

And life be for reservations

    Living with adversity

4

AWE is tender wonder

Straining to enlighten!

As lightening brings on thunder,

Is sometimes cause to frighten

5

To explore the lore of uncertainty

To reject all this, to refute,

To question all virility,

To AWE as absolute!

6

In him that made the eyes to see,

Knew from patient testing

How to respect his growing tree

With appreciation's blessing

7

This is, as in our lives, a world

Of magnificent creation

And as AWE lies stiffly unfurled,

Never exceeding explanation.

H E BRIGHT
3/22/14
apls

THE REAL
STRING THEORY

From tossed dice to a shuffled deck,

    Outcomes get prearranged

Something is controlling every aspect,

    Of our lives, and is often changed

2

Sailing on life, as an uncharted tour

    Usually with good intensions,

Perhaps pre-determined and bartered for,

    Or blindly with strange interventions

3

Without expectation for waves crashing

    Could drown as one goes,

With unknown destinations often clashing,

    On a course not pre-disposed

4

AT THE BEGINNING, upon arrival

The chosen was selected to reside

And strict revisions for survival

Were given, and provisions supplied

5

But with ideals distorted

Sorts in confusion

Appeals contorted,

Thoughts, as illusion

6

And stranger yet, for every bout,

Wrestled from frivolous things,

OMENS were presented, as signs without doubt

"Something was pulling our strings"

7

For ideas were requested,

 Suddenly shown the light

Better solutions were suggested,

 That to us, came as insight

8

And bright lights were binding,

 For halos of glowing rings,

Accepting guidance, annoyed, finding

 Someone pulling our strings

9

With arrogance unsightly,

 A correction of things

Like errors, even slightly,

 Needed alignment of strings

10

Unwittingly agreed

    For corrections not planned

Adjustments to proceed

    Pulling strings, helped to understand.

H Ebright
4/14/14

4 OJ

THE PURSUIT FOR HUMANITY IS LOVE

AS A TREATABLE MALADY

OFTEN CURED WITH MARRIAGE — {OR CARRIAGE}

Love is an emotion, a notion,

    For tender stimulation,

It supplies the potion for devotion,

    And the lotion for motion!

Love requires desires and concessions,

    As restrictions can insist,

On obligations, and expressions,

    Whatever compassion can't resist.

And lust to become a mindless blunder,

    With confusion, in a maze

Lost, as an experience of wonder.

    An experimental phase.

Love as not how you fake it

    For acceptance, so often unclear,

But as fidelity, one might sake it,

    To not undo it all in fear.

Deep and pure love, as so rare,

    Could BE with anything.

For nothing can compare,

    With a real heart-felt offering.

So! By any love you try,

Be it for Gal or Guy or why

For all too soon is "Bye-Bye,"

    As just one left to sigh,

Harold E. 4/26/14

A WORDLY WINDOW

Elbows sore, propped on a sill,

    Embracing a ruddy chin,

In her sagging seat of fiberfill,

    Her home, is nestled in

2

Never could a sadder sister

    Whittle time, to waste

Threading a life's lethargic vista,

    Almost alive, but her space

3

As a good seat,

    Is a centered, front row casualty

Dissolved in defeat,

    Resolved in apathy.

4

Down on her luck,

  From the beginning

Wrought, as if hell had struck,

  Condemning a life, for sinning

5

Her face is anguish, hardly resting

  Fuming with resent,

Like when wine is spit out, after testing,

  Wasting the ferment.

6

A flattened brow, presses the pane,

  Cold in concentration,

 With thoughts of just being can sustain,

  A minimum of participation

7

Impulsions seed a loser's

    Need for pleasures

Worsened more by self abusers

    Who consider those as treasures.

8

Flickering lights mimic the sea,

    On her frozen window pane,

As headlights swirl her world, to be

    One living inhumane

9

With a frozen window, as a shipping line

    Sailing only at request

Fueled cheap, on potent wine

    Only worsened to suggest -

10

How elbows, mired with visions cast,

    And elations not encouraging

The wine poured does not last,

    As reality comes discouraging

11

For only with booze

    Demanding dreams to cruise,

She, Having nothing - has nothing to lose,

    Leaves for only emptiness, to chose

12

Her worldly window, sadly shocking

    Leaves her dreaming, waiting alone,

If a conscience can come knocking,

    It could bring something to atone.

OMINOUS CLOUDS

Ominous clouds, puffy darkened forms
    Carried rain and rusty debris
Made the land from dusty storms,
    And the piles of sand we see,

2

For millions of years, pebbled rain
    Seeded the land and grounds
Kneaded the sand tight, every grain,
    Till mountains rose from mounds

3

Raining springs of purified nectar
    Flowed from ancient pores,
Mother nature's magic sepulcher
    Gives us earth and all because,

4

Appreciation as an obligation

    Made is readily to conserve,

That without deliberation,

    Of a trust, a cause to preserve

5

Mountains have stood and precious land

    From a mother who cared,

For those too understand,

    How she labored, shaped and prepared,

6

For a promise from maternity

    Gave up an earth to share,

Said, for all eternity,

    Has a bed that all will wear.

H Ebright

4/9/14

SICK AGAIN

Gaspingly with nothing said,

Complaining sickly being shed,

Sneezingly with bugs to spread,

Germs to see a seasons dread.

Sick again, got the flu,

Steeping tea and scalding brew,

A painful case has nothing new,

To trash this bug with options few.

Trundles too, on chamber pots,

Flying high on NyQuil shots,

Dripping, sniffing nasal snots,

Ain't no way, getting the hots.

Fever sweating an uprising,

    Now one-o-two and realizing

Didn't avoid is not surprising,

    A doctored mirror, not disguising

Virus caught me, what a bitch,

    Luckily no twitch or itch,

Prayed, amen perhaps to switch,

    Time, comes time without a switch.

Stay perhaps, relapse in surrender,

    Any way, as a contender

Mindful, just to remember,

    Either way, rough or tender

H.Ebright 6/23/14

BUGGED

Got bugged somehow painfully,

    Sneezing wheezing relentlessly

Drugged numb, a certainty,

    Reasoning for such irony

Downed anew with options few,

    In steeping tea and scalding brew,

A creeping case of nothing new,

    Again, to chase a bugging flu,

A grasping soreness viral spread,

    A painful strain, one to dread,

A rasping aching spiral head,

    As gainful wrath, one path ahead

Trundle trots, to chamber pots

    Flying high on NyQuil shots,

Sniffing, dripping nasal snots,

    Hell-of-a-way for getting hot

Sweating fever, as an up rise,

   One-O-two to realize

Did not avoid, as no surprise,

   A doctored mirror can't disguise

Virus needed someone, the Bitch,

   Found in me, the perfect hitch,

Luckily no twitch or itch,

   So bound to Here, her time to switch

H EBRIGHT
7/1/14

A HOME TO GROW ON

To grow by the sea, and understand,

    How yesterday dissolves,

Settled a land of white clean sand,

    As tomorrow's seed to evolves

Where dunes form at winds command,

    To crest with salted foam,

To wonder if a tidal hand,

    Suggests a nascent home.

Prayed for, by people who appreciate,

    Being a contender

Graying to remember to congratulate,

    Those who wouldn't surrender

With nothing certain climate churns,

    Behind weather's curtain, lessons are
    learned.

To live with trauma, spaced to stay,

    Plagued by drama with everything earned.

From Montauk to Manhattan bay,

Life fulfilled in a special way.

Islanders, not the teams

Deserving demands, conserving lands,

Crystals of granules panned,

Measures of pleasures tenderly planned,

Long Islanders treasure their sands.

H Ebright

7/14/14

A PLACE FOR HOME

A hundred billion stars and more
   In this galaxy alone,
Trillions of bodies, no one's sure,
   For a place we all call home.

A million, million galaxies observed,
   Astronomical in size,
Has a tiny space reserved,
   As that, to colonize

For relativity, an expression,
   Is a circle standing unclosed
Looped end to end, as a suggestion.
   To satisfy reposed.

Then getting pushed from bed one night,

    She needing space and more.

Awoke startled, me out of sight,

    Found on the floor.

Adjustment is space, often desired

    Depending on circumstance,

As deep concentration is required

    If all this be nothing but trance

Conscience is sight to always be

    That of light, as only we

With the possibility,

    To stay our right for responsibility

Is there, how one can see

    That which is here Perhaps not

As only observation makes it be,

    So gifted are we, as creations lot.

And from the floor unperturbed,

To disappear when sight disturbs

That as being unobserved,

Is only what the mind conserves.

H EBRIGHT

8/1/14/ AS

ONE EARTH ONLY

Age comes to time the new generation

   With obligations

So in passing to give the earth roses,

   For preservations

Sadly for our kids inheriting anxiety

   As massive technologies and data

Stage for authority rage for priority

Stunted buds cripples roses

   Depriving bees of nectar

Young indecisions unjust, I suppose

   As crowds resent the specter.

Igniting a candle to believe,

   In protecting a mother,

When she receives

   Disrespect to smother.

Every generation designs

    As history assigns sometimes tears

Changes are for preserving minds,

    And hasn't changed a thousand years

H Ebright   9 10 14

TO SEASONED YEARS

A seasoning for years to stage

    That, which underscores

The reasoning for tears that rage

    At times, when life ignores.

Spring has so kindly traded freezes

    Of winter's cold and blue

To changing airs, on tender breezes

    Warming blessings overdue.

Teased with committed wheezes,

    For sunrays overview

Winter is it's best when thawing,

    Springing to pause his rages

Summer sees to his fad, ignoring

    Our turning calendar pages

Now piling up mounds of leaves blow,
　　The winds in trees displace
　Grounds freezing dew to show,
　　　Frozen webs of lace.

In fall each crunching step makes
　　For bunching natures green,
　The piles of mountain leaves to rake,
　　　Are blowing summers scenes

Fall is freezing the pumpkin's rind
　　Where tempeture requests,
To never leave the best behind
　　　Wasted, as nature suggests

Season abounds as reason confounds
　　For enjoying all that life allows
Respecting that, when living astounds
　　　Those aging kindly, as time avows

H EBRIGHT
10/13/14
4 applesauce

WHEN IS LIFE BEST

Spring so kindly changes the season,
Rearranges thaw from freeze,
Occasionally pausing time to reason
So weather can appease

Abiding, as the season aging,
Easing tears discord,
Denying fears as wild storms raging
Appeasing lives restored.

Winter folds best, when thawing,
Spring molds props in stages
Summer is boldly ignoring
Time, turning calendar pages

Summer lives as the drummers beat
　　Keeps strumming for the purse,
As those with much invested cheat,
　　To chase the waiting hearse

Fall mounds leaf piles stowing talks
　　Crunching nature scenes,
Miles for raking trails for walks
　　Restraining summer greens.

Fall to shape the pumpkins round
　　Where temperament suggests
Life so formed, has finally found
　　Fulfillments to express

Seasons confuse reasons to excuse
　　Enjoyments, when yield coincides
Respecting life, as taking abuse,
　　Aging kindly when time decides

Grown each season, aged for reason

Prone to deter of the reaper

The final time, in any season,

Can atone with the master keeper.

H.E bright

10/21/2014
aplsas

A SEA SEES LIFE

As muster calls with the rising sun

A father pays the oceans dun,

Trusting in fate for a special one,

With payment for his only son,

    To set upon the sea, a course,

    Providing for this lad,

    To sail instead, as in sad remorse,

    The life he wished he had.

As adventurers in sighting krill

See blowing fountains, spraying.

Earning each lesson, though however frill

Observing whales displaying.

    Soon weather threatens and seas loom,

    No raging storm ever behaves,

    Assuming such as potential doom,

    Envisioning watery graves.

Riggings fail, pushed by screaming storms,

Sterns howl in mountainous swells,

Heaving sterns growl dipping rails

An ocean trashing expels,

>Building character, born of dangerous
>shoals,
>
>When rough seas overwhelm,
>
>Gambling with death, and for goals
>
>Staking on those men, heroes, who helm.

Sharing uncertainties, the seas was chose,

Engaging an ocean outraged,

Bailed every tear, unkindly exposed

As each drop weighed blindly outraged

>Preparing for the calmer tiding
>
>Heading for higher shores,
>
>With beds of down shallows residing
>
>For any place drier, without oars.

Setting the anchor one last time

Treading time at waters edge,

Drawing breaths of salted brine,

Trading it all, for his coral ledge.

So shorn from a spiritual hand,

Heaved wrought from due respect,

So fathered now lain, made the Man,

On his solid ground standing erect.

H Ebright
9/16/14

LENORE

Kept a gal, a HEALER pal

   Who used music's floes to feel

For patient's woes, she tenderly chose

   With hands of peace to heal,

So past the years, began with fears

   No one bodies, immune

Progressions lessons strife, too many tears

   Has God's permission to commune.

Suggesting now, as with resting how

   Having paid the life time's dues,

For peace the kind, for a special mind

   You can cure you, with all my blessings

Harold 10/6/14

THE ORCHARD

A farmer sees his orchard down
    As wind and hail collide
He wells when deep devotion found
    His emotion, gripping pride

It wasn't the storm that drained
    His orchard's fertile land,
It was prearranged, and oddly aimed,
    That he might understand
How five generations past, believed
    That growing trees wore treasures
And knew how apple spirits conceived
    Would ripen with hapless pleasures.

All TREES were blighted sick and felled

    As had nature decided to choose

One granted pardon, was not expelled

    Surviving with nothing to lose.

Where from acres tearful inspection

    Came an inspired miracle's splendor

Had left one tree, denying rejection,

    Gifted as blight resistant gender.

As sighs of pain, soothed demanding

    With summer all but lost

Replanted trees from that single standing,

    All blessed by that special force.

Out of insistence from nature's wrath,

    Given lineage from that tree,

Found on a predetermined path,

    The progenitor of rare serendipity

Cuttings sprung, and new trees grew

  Five years hence to fruit.

So proudly blessed, with instinct knew

  How budding prayers take root

Before times strip, seasons call

Before wine powers ferment

Before binds grip, reasons stall

Before mind cowers, content.

When desperations came as losses

  Inspirations fill the day,

Irritation's pent up, forces

  Intimidations, dents will splay.

Preparations meant, as crosses

  Trepidation scents, dismay.

Happinesses as lent, to applesauces.

     H. Ebright 11/11/14

POETIC DILEMMAS

Inspirations caused the pen in hand, to understand how imperfection could never be in

Command of ideograms, and a cause for words to caress thoughts and express how warts might be beneficial for a toad, (So says the frog.) For writers in a fog-

Ideas come from anywhere and everywhere at the same time, as leaves (pages) forced from thee, are to become as residue from what once could have been a tree. As a concept starts at the rear to perceive a beginning, spinning a center is relieved in either direction as has to be conceived, to be believed.

Ramps to stairways, steps to airways, marking tracts as a pad of facts, engaged for inspiration, obligingly stacks the packs, sought to soften the written thought of complexity in variation.

As a stagnant dead bird withers with the stench of obscurity, workings bold, (all too often as maturity) get sold as masterpieces, but only for security.

So are the poetic dilemmas of the poet, determined to weather the storms of obscurity.

HAROLD E.
12/10/14

TO SEE AS A BEE

A buzzing bee hangs, web entwined
    Fears for his life being annihilated
For what purpose had nature designed,
    This predestined course so violated.

He shuffles uselessly, wrapped tightly
    Struggles to negotiate a deal.
With life on the line all too likely,
    Considered as bee spider meal.

An invisible net binds unwary guests
    Caught as in devious ploys.
Sought as a predator's instinct suggests,
    They remain as dinner, a diner enjoys.

Had the bee flew elsewhere instead,

    Could not as a meal, been trapped,

As grim these binds of silken thread,

    So bound as body's wrapt.

The bee concedes being seduced,

    As prey he conceivably detains-

The spider's hunger, though never reduced,

    When his dinner now hanging, explains-

"I make the honey, and pollinate,

    For your web might never be,

Without this branch, to habitate,

    Could never have caught me."

The spider wiped five teary eyes,

    Saw in a bee, strength and qualm

But not once to apologize,

    For too shortly will embalm.

So only with life, is one to assume,

How tragically sadness comes true.

Nature concedes to never presume

When spiders do, as spiders do.

H Ebright
12/4/14

THE HOUSE OF

A drunk rang the bell for Willey the fruit,
    He ran a brothel, of ill repute
There women callous and very astute,
    Knew how perfection will execute,

As a house to evolve, per tradition,
    And resolve that tranquility be essential,
The want for normalcy to be a condition,
    But never dreamed of strife's potential.

Business mending special parts,
    Lending for peace somehow fleeting
Where girls vending exotic arts,
    Tending broken hearts, bleeding.

Harmony stays when time that moves

    Can hone an edge, improving grooves

As when perfection, somewhat behooves,

    For a life with strife, never soothes.

 A fight ensued, and a woman went,

    Thrown from a window, as an irate gent

Caused her to splatter, on hard cement,

    Prone to shatter, bounced and spent

HE screams at the sight, a straggler yells

    A drunken sot tripped and fell,

Aghast at how as a body swells

    Could last the night, he dares to dwell.

Crocked and shocked at half past four,

    His staggers, knocking at Willies door,

To perhaps earn, for one good chore,

    The sum as all conscience, too explore.

Glassy eyed unclothed, came Will,

    Spied this drunk, who stunk of swill

Could barely vent his anger fill,

    Uncloaked beyond an embittered pill.

The drunken bumpkin, insisting he found,

    For that witch lying on the ground

With speculated words, very profound,

    Said, "Sir I think your SIGN fell down."

This house of business in Willie's care

    As this tale might humble one with flair,

A girl did fall, though filled with AIR,

    Was for half off, as a bargainer's dare .....

H Ebright
12/16/14

CHAPTER 6

The Goodbye: 2015

The Goodbye

Although Harold did not want to be alone, he wanted to be where he considered home. His search was now for someone to take care of him.

Not long before he passed away, he said he was feeling old, and this was new to him. I see the poems of this period convey the shortness of time he believes he had remaining. The poems seem to be the most defined, or easiest to understand of all his work.

The night before he passed away, he was busy working on a poem. It is the last poem in this book. Was it his goodbye? Did he know it was one of his last days here? He awoke to feeling not well. (He didn't have the best heart connections). And before he reached the hospital, he was gone.

More important than any of his poems, the six lines of this beginning of a poem, to me, befit the end of his life and his poetry.

NO STRANGER WILL

Thanking the lords,

   Whatever they are

Scrutinizing our accords,

   Inspecting our star.

For we as humans, are restrained by lines

   And unfortunately hung on strings.

As when others decide for our lives and minds,

   Will provide where and what fate brings.

Just who are these others to make decisions,

   And reject our reality,

Correcting our conclusions, with their
provisions,

   Selecting as their partiality

They augment our ability

    And lead us to supplement.

  As their illusions of stability,

    Proclaim to re-invent —

Newer renditions, invade our souls

    Persuading us to participate.

Apart from our selected goals,

    We strain to deviate.

Bent to placate and dispose,

    As most ironic, they impose

A manipulation that was chose,

    For us as tonic, they suppose.

Called angels, guides, perhaps troubadours,

    With songs to captivate,

Their projection soars in ways and laws

    Bending wills to cultivate.

And for that to sound, to part our lives,

As instrumental from their vibes,

Sustaining our niches, there one survives,

With momentum as riches, for our hives

H Ebright 1/8/15

AGENIES

I SPIED A ROSE, DENIED OF FAME

DRAWN WITHERED, DOSEN'T EXPLAIN

LIMPING FLICKERING LIFE AS A FLAME.

HAD TWICE SO CHOSE, TO LOVE AS BANE

TO POUNCE UPON A LOG, AND TAME

THE LAUGH THE LOVE, AS LIT HER
FLAME.

SO PRIED A ROSE, CRIED OF SHAME,

TO FIND, AS RIVERS TIMELY WANE

THE FLOE, AS GOES DISGUISING FEIGN

CAN POSE TO EXPOSE, BEING VAIN

AT STRESSING LOVE, AS MIGHT CONTAIN

A DEPRESSED ROSE FOR MEMORIES
STAIN

I DEFIED THE ROSE, COMPLIED IN
BLAME

SO SAID OF WOWS, DENIED OF FAME,

TO SHED THE LOES RELIED ON GAIN

AS EVER TO GRAY THE SPINAL MANE

AND THEN, ASTRIDE THE FINIAL PAIN

FOREVERS ONE ASIDE CAN'T EXPLAIN.

HAROLD E.
1/10/15/

APPLESAUCES

THE RIVER

1

In flows in trickles, and combines
    On the floors of wooded land.
There bubbles perking leafy brines
    Are awed by water's demand

2

From a shallow crook of earth
    Spews purity seldom found,
As emerging magic, such is birth
    Now springing hallowed ground-

3

As an artisan belching wonder
    Forms a harrow gripping sand,
Spreading showers of the thunder,
    Treading narrows in the land

4

Down a leafy crested hill

  It cascades, percolating,

Conforming as a tiny rill

  These waters incubating.

5

Now a gushing stream emerging

  Leeching on the scene,

Deepening banks, as water purging

  Has matched the velvet green.

6

Contented trees where all who bed

  Have liquids to embrace,

And woodland creatures dare to tread

  So trued by nature's grace.

7

A heady stream now fills requests

    Fed bounties from the skies,

When from a sliver one suggests,

    "That's a river from disguise."

8

No need on earth more precious

    Where the feel of velvet waters,

Can heal, in the last of freshness

    When at brackish ocean borders

9

For now the water in deciding,

    Yet a thousand whiles to chase,

The flows for chasms widening

    And shows an enchanted face –

10

That appeals for cloudy mists to rise

　And waits till newer storms provide

The seeds for clouds to energize,

　　Then rains for a river are not denied

H Ebright
1/29/15

A HOME SWEET HOME

As rust the scourge of irons might

    So purge life's every second,

Where dust to cover wrinkles, light

    Shines through, as twilight beckoned

Innumerable bodies, probably more

    Is a universe to grace

A trillion stars, no one's sure

    A confident of space.

As dusts and rusts dull brightening,

    On a blackboard's blackened sky

Each glows a sun enlightening,

    So strewn, perfecting ply

Overhead, as grand the spread,

    Of stars from end to end

So is wondrous for us imbed

    To contemplate and tend –

And realize, of such enormity

    And a plausible reflection

To find a causeable conformity,

    For a "Rest in peace" expression

Beings, as a fact of being

    Making sense of why,

For only, as in the act of seeing,

    Is staking every reason to try.

H E BRIGHT 2/2/15

**From
Mary**

TINY TOES 2

I woke in irony, chasing thought,
    Conspiring as a whim,
To have acquired, as so long sought,
    Fulfilled my desires for him –

2

Tiny toes, paws in a fur ball
    A pink nose twitching forlorn,
His mother's nudging is first to call,
    For a thirsting puppy just born.

3

It dawns on me each morning,
    As living wears away from birth,
How ageing dares each year dawning,
    To make life, equal to worth.

4

Into my world this puppy came,

From good stock, idolized

Born from winners proclaiming fame,

Bred as champions, prized.

5

Bequeathed beneath a family tree

For chanting to explore

A lineage granting pedigree,

Is to yearn, and to cry for more.

6

Born complete, shorn to compete

He finds me his "god and guide"

To justify, and cause conceit

Encouraging us, side by side.

7

Where only as an uncoupled train,

    Can ever achieve,

For that to never separate gain,

    As one, we best receive.

8

Four paws and loveliness growing,

    To flaunt, at fans command

As our best is proudly showing

    How blue ribbons meet demand.

9

So ripe for competition

    When discretion is required,

Our plight, apart from contradiction

    Has perfection most desired

10

We shook the top off circumstance,

    As the heart of the crowd propels

Two winners, defying chance

    And our cause to bind, excels

11

Thus for fame as precious, came

    Our time for gold assigned,

As stressed we told elations shame,

    Of the love we hold, combined.

12

When first we needed stations high

    To force a cause that thrilled

And so as fame did justify,

    Our destiny's fulfilled,

13

A partnership proudly found

    The best known and so timed

To test a lifetime most profound,

    In greatness, for peace of mind

14

Happiness extended our lives

    And companionship allowed

Extra years in potential strives

    As we possessed the crowd

H Ebright
5/5/15

A Clock in Time

In unrealistic basic form
Is metal ore refined
Until a fate congeals its shape
The holders hand defined.

A wealth of parts a stealth of hearts
Conceive a plan that's sure
To form the tarts in kitchen starts
Mechanically a – lure

As clocks are tolls machinery pools
Assembled cogs and wheels
Wherever scattered jumbles rule
The makers biggest deals

Who handle time couldn't start

    A master of degrees

    For clocks and time are worlds apart

    As seed create the trees

    When all the parts are timely honed

    And snugly fitten then

    A counter parted episode

    Can thus begin again

    Where comes the right to be correct

    What ever the condition

    If broken parts seek less respect

    Time honors no petition

    For this relationship with man

    Has cause to seek alarm

    For us the deft escapement plan

    Is books of prayers and psalms

So all is geared to oil as planned

In everything we match-up

The craftman's hand with grease demands

A universal catch-up

With unrelentless ticks and tocks

And universes fly

Why choose to see all other clocks

As visions in the sky ....

H.E. Bright

I CAN'T BELIEVE IT

There are a many basic questions about the universe that have scientists scratching their heads, looking for plausible answers.

Due to complexity attributed to an explanation, some questions are better off not answered, especially if no reasonable understandings are at this time. If I may, I'd like to think in uncomplicated terms and with all the basics.

Evaluations might be easier, thinking in simple, sensible and perhaps understandable for situations. It all comes out confusing anyway.

Four questions that obligate the hearts of scientists everywhere. Such as:

What makes the world go around?

How does gravity hold everything together?

Is motion the culprit that has to do with everything known?

And just how dark could dark matter be?

To begin with facts of great importance:

With every action there is generated an equal or grander action, usually in the opposite direction. For every push, there is a pull. With every up is a down. And for every future there is a past.

How come every moving object in space establishes rotation. Subatomic particles coming in proximity with one another start a circulation, a rotation, probably caused by this entire cosmos circulating around the most massive (as yet not detected) black black hole. The expansion of the universe is probably not expansion at all, but rather everything (everything) circulating.

Stated simply:

Water's downward flow circulates. Mountains of high-pressure air, as in meteorology, have a center with the greatest mass circling. Earth circling the sun, and spinning. Spinning objects create forces in two directions. One outward, and the opposite force pushing inward compressing the center. A combination of the two, so balanced, that only nature with its fantastic ability to have, and have not, do we exist at all.

Everything in nature comes out even, Sooner or later. Both subatomic particles and black holes are affected, and the phantom being labeled as Dark Matter, or neutrinos, is not matter at all, but rather the opposite of centrifugal forces. Gravity is not a particle, but rather a force to be considered as an opposition to any circulation.

Sent the kids out to the backyard swimming pool to clean it out, all they did was to start a fast moving rotation around the outsides of the pool water. Which in effect caused all the garbage to accumulate in the center. The faster they rotated the water, the sooner the stuff gathered to the center. Had they been able to go fast enough, the accumulating material would have left the pool. Now how basic can that be, as an example of material spewing out of black holes now.

Lows, in weather, do not exist. Actually, they are there because of an absence of high pressure masses of air. Given the earth's spin they become areas of high pressure, with the greatest amount of air accumulating in the center (areas of high pressure) Just what force drags everything to its center? Look in a quasar circulating at almost the speed of light shooting out tremendous amounts of accumulated debris millions of light years in space.

The speed of matter circulating in a black hole almost surpasses the boundaries of predicted possibility. Quasars are the best example of this force in nature.

Gravity is not a BOSON particle, but a reactive force against the force of the centrifugal. A very naturally occurring reaction in all of nature and everything, EVERYTHING rotates. Here is everything spinning and creating the opposite directional push inward towards the center of its spin. Imagine the forces exerted inward, in an object rotating beyond the speed of light. Such could be the scenario in every black hole.

And why then, with a theory of the expansion of the universe do the galaxies themselves not elongate in space, but progressively, very slowly migrate towards the center, balanced again by the two opposing forces in nature.

Math is not an absolute science where nature is concerned. For example, consider a falling object not ever able to reach a predetermined destination because, mathematically its remaining distance can always (mathematically) be halved, and never reach.

A yard is the distance between ones measuring chin and his thumb. Whomsoever measures.

I watched a duck in a pond swimming around in a circle, bringing up food from the bottom of the water. Is there an intelligence there, or just dumb duck luck?

WITH HOPE AND THE BEST FOR LIFE

With hope and the better possibility for the best life has to offer. The aspirations of thousands for the fulfillment of dreams, and what life has to offer, as the wishes for living good. If this be reality, then what I hold in my hand could make dreams come true. To change one's being forever more. THIS IS A WISH BONE, and only through one's mental capacity could things change. There is always hope for the best that life has to offer. For the fulfillment of dreams. Actually, it wasn't so lucky for the chicken. But she too fulfilled her destiny.

Throw in some hope — luck — and the ability to be with all things in a world of possible realities. That means nothing is as it seems... Take for example a million dollar Pablo Picasso painting— No two people out of millions see the work the same. Or interpret it likewise. Which actually gives us individually, Thank goodness, and the ability to be one with the universe. Not only do we live in the best of times (technologally), but under the most impossible circumstances to be here at all seeing how...

My daughter Kim, Age 3 had the right idea that sort of jumpstarted This kind of thinking about what reality is.

Whenever I would get on her case about something or whatever, she would cover her eyes, and poof: I was GONE.

As the subject for this discussion is how can one interpret what is real and what is superficially possible, when even the most advanced scientific minds cannot explain what consciousness is. 20,000 people hear a poem, see art, and there are literally 20 thousand different versions in people's minds. So it simply comes down to what is real and what is not. What is PLOT and what is ROT coming down to interaction with interpretation.

Back to Kim, age 3. In her view, she saw what things really were as her view. So I asked this 3 year old to explain and she said "With her eyes closed I went away, and she argued that she didn't. And with her eyes hidden I'm not there, and everything I'm saying is not real either. I argued, you can touch me with your eyes closed, and she said, "Only if I find you — And only if I choose too"

Well she floored me with that which meant she was choosing her own reality.

So what actually is consciousness? In one simple word (Which there isn't) it is awareness of reality, and what is reality? Well awareness if visual, mental, sensual, The multitude of the seven senses. Yes! There are even more yet undiscovered in the quantum field of science which has become the enigma of science today.

All questions are simple if you know the answers. But not all answers are understandable. Simple things like, "What is dark matter, or dark energy?" Things that are only possible should they exist at all. These are the things that our lives hinge upon for existence making reality what is, or might be.

GOODBYE

I am somewhere & will always be

No matter what, unfortunately

If ashes, or bone, or thoughts are me

Perhaps, to fertilize a tree

Since I once was

I can never not be

H.E. Bright
5/12/2013

www.ingramcontent.com/pod-product-compliance
Lightning Source LLC
La Vergne TN
LVHW051357080426
835508LV00022B/2866